ADDITIONAL PRAISE FOR
KEEPING SCORE WITH GRITT

"Firsthand, I watched and benefitted as Shawn started then built PFSbrands into the record-setting success it is today. As a supplier from the beginning, we shipped an initial order of one hundred pounds via UPS, and just ten years later PFSbrands had a fleet of trucks that were at our dock picking up one hundred thousand pounds every month.

Shawn's book explains how everyone can use his core values, principles, tools, and methods, which have guided PFSbrands toward its twentieth consecutive year of double-digit growth and an unbelievable run of nine straight years on the Inc. 5000 list of fastest-growing privately held companies. Both a fascinating story and invaluable set of tools to live and work by."

STEVEN HOLTSCLAW

President, Texas Crumb and Food Products

"Seventeen months into my new position and I am privileged to work directly for Shawn! It has been an exciting and mind-spinning change of culture! Coming from a completely different culture, I have been pleasantly surprised by the experience of Open-Book Management. Being able to work through budgets and daily business practices with the entire team brings together the straight talk and hands-on experience that is necessary in achieving a greater working knowledge of the company's goals! PFSbrands' culture also includes a different example of goal setting. Utilizing our very own GRITTrac system, which holds us accountable, is a welcome change during my workday. I am excited to put all of the tools provided by Shawn and this amazing company into practice!"

LAURA LAUNE

Business Manager, Burcham Companies

"Over the course of many years, I have been associated with PFSbrands as a wholesale partner. I have always valued and trusted the insight, advice, and wisdom that Shawn has provided at times when I've needed and asked for it. He is a thoughtful listener, a straight shooter, and a man of moral integrity. Both his life and business are a clear reflection of his core values. The drive and determination he puts forth to continuously evolve is awe inspiring. His business acumen is visionary. His leadership skills are exemplary. His can-do attitude is contagious.

I'm proud to call Shawn both a friend and mentor. This book is sure to be an enormous asset to people of all levels of business who are striving for success."

ALLISON CHAPMAN

Regional Manager, Lyons Specialty Company

"Without a doubt, Shawn Burcham is a true trailblazer. I've watched his company's remarkable GRITT-based culture in action for five years. The results are undeniable. Who knew how treating employees like true co-owners (or making them co-owners) could lead to such phenomenal growth and financial success?"

CARL CHRISTENSON

Retired VP of Marketing, PFSbrands; Marketing Consultant

"In the thirty years I've known Shawn, he has always been a leader. 'Straight talk' describes Shawn's leadership style well. From our time in college, to my employment at PFSbrands, and beyond, I've always sought Shawn's advice on how to obtain success. It's great that he has finally written this book!"

BRETT HORN

"In business, and life for that matter, knowing where you stand with someone is critical. Shawn Burcham's dedication to 'straight talk communication' to all the people in his life, coworkers, vendors, customers, and even family is just one of the reasons PFSbrands grew from his garage in Willard, Missouri, to become one of the fastest-growing privately held companies in America.

Through a commitment to self-improvement by setting tangible goals, relentless practice, and lifelong learning, Shawn and Julie Burcham took it one step further by transferring 100 percent of ownership to PFSbrands' employees in an ESOP. By any standard, this should be the definition of the 'American Dream.'

Keeping Score with GRITT: Straight Talk Strategies for Success is a window into Shawn Burcham's practical insights, systems, and beliefs, which have made him a highly effective leader, business owner, and now coach to other leaders aspiring to achieve similar results. I'd encourage every leader who wants to get to the next level to study Shawn's book and life."

WILL SNOOK
Founder and CEO, Traffic Safety Store

"*Keeping Score with GRITT: Straight Talk Strategies for Success* is a fun, no-nonsense approach to business and life. Shawn's 'straight talk' about his hard-earned lessons and successes distill the daunting challenges faced by today's entrepreneurs, business owners, leaders, and employees down into simple, actionable items that everyone can relate to and implement. Regardless of your industry, stage of your career, or organization size, we can all benefit from some extra GRITT."

JAIR DROOGER
CT Assist

"As I reflect on our seven-year relationship with PFSbrands, one characteristic rises above all others: culture. It's amazing, it's contagious, and if you have the honor of touring their facility you want more of it. A prime example of this feeling was during a recent Discovery Days event attended by myself and one of our key accounts. For those of you who haven't attended, Discovery Days is a fast-paced two-day introduction to PFSbrands. During breakfast on day two, I asked my client for his thoughts. He said, 'Ali, I couldn't sleep last night. I have to find a way to do business with these people.' He didn't say their products are great, which they are. He didn't say their processes are great, which they are, nor did he say their support is fantastic, which it is. He said PEOPLE. The PEOPLE are what he remembered and was impressed by most. What more can I say? The culture Shawn Burcham has created is the cornerstone of his success. We couldn't be prouder to be a part of it."

ALI MOMENZADEH
CSO, Lyons Specialty Company

"Congratulations, Shawn and PFSbrands! Shawn and I are going on thirty years of a friendship that I truly value and that I believe the foundation of which is due to sharing the core values that he lays out in chapter 1 of *Keeping Score with GRITT.* There was never a doubt that Shawn and Julie would be extremely successful in any endeavor they pursued. All the accomplishments and accolades are deserved. I was excited to hear about the book a couple of months ago and now I can't wait to see how many people will be positively impacted by it!"

L. CHAD BURTON, DDS
CAPT, DC, USN

"My time here at PFSbrands is summed up with one word: wow! Shawn and I met in 2001 and have never looked back. There have been ups and downs and both good ideas and some ideas we should have never thought of. But it was always about how we could help our customers and employees become more successful at home and at work.

As one of only a few employees in 2001 we could be considered the receptionist, warehouse worker, driver, salesperson, trainer, marketing rep, show person, purchasing agent, and about anything else you can think of that was needed. Today we have multiple brands, multiple companies, franchisees, and multiple options for our retailers. PFSbrands has grown to over 140 employee-owners and I'm proud to have witnessed it from near the beginning.

I do miss the old days, but through it all Shawn has always believed in taking care of the customer, the company, and the employees and doing what we said we would do. Shawn has worked hard to set up Open-Book Management so everyone in the company can see the sales, the expenses, and the 'bottom line' profits. Open-Book Management helps people to see the big picture and it's helped PFSbrands scale.

Shawn has grown PFSbrands with grit and vision. His leadership has led to substantial growth and a great future for our customers and EOs (employee -owners). He has been a mentor and friend for eighteen years and I could not recommend a better read than Shawn's book for your company and employees to succeed.

My success over the last eighteen years has been a result of Shawn giving me the tools I needed and me using them."

DARRELL HALE
Retired Senior Leader, PFSbrands

"People are attracted to those whom are highly successful both personally and professionally. How did they become so successful? Shawn Burcham has developed his business skills and strategies throughout his career. He is focused not just on his own success, but the success of his customers, employees, and community. Such success is achieved via the application of his work ethic, perseverance, years of work experiences, personable interaction with customers, and long-term focus. Get to know Shawn better and find out how he plans for and achieves success."

TOM GODDARD

Dairy Farmers of America (Retired)

"Shawn and I have been friends for over twenty-five years. We met in college when I was fortunate to be accepted into the fraternity that Shawn belonged to. I felt like I hit the jackpot when Shawn selected me as his pledge son, as I gained a great mentor. We have remained friends since college and our friendship strengthened when Shawn's family moved from Willard, Missouri, to the Jefferson City, Missouri, area. Shawn and I have always enjoyed talking about business. I have always respected and admired his work ethic and the culture he has created at PFSbrands. In July of 2017, we entered a new venture together as partners in a lawn-care business. Our goal is to create a culture where core values, straight talk, and Open-Book Management will make us a great place to work in today's environment. With Shawn's mentoring and with the help of the GRITT Business Coaching team, we have begun to transform a twenty-year-old irrigation business into our vision. There are only a few people I have met in my life with such a positive outlook on life and business. Shawn is one of these people."

CHRIS JORDAN

President, All-n-One Outdoor Solutions

"We started doing business with PFSbrands in the fall of 2007. I met Shawn at the Pace Show in Missouri and was very interested in his Champs Chicken program. One of the comments I made after talking to him throughout the show was that he spent a lot of time 'interviewing' me on our company. I found that very interesting, but once I got to know him and his company I completely understood where he was coming from. He holds everyone that touches his business to a very high standard, which I believe has made him and PFSbrands so successful! Shawn has built a team at PFSbrands that is compared to none in our industry that will insure their continued success. Shawn has always been one of our very best 'partners' and I appreciate all of he has done for us!"

RICK VANCE

VP of Marketing, AMCON Distributing Company

"As the cofounder, architect, and leader of a truly great company, Shawn Burcham has been racking up winning scores for more than twenty years. Follow the advice in this practical—and insightful—book, and your scores will start rising as well."

BO BURLINGHAM

Author, Small Giants *and* Finish Big

KEEPING SCORE WITH GRITT™

SHAWN BURCHAM

KEEPING SCORE WITH GRITT™

STRAIGHT TALK STRATEGIES FOR SUCCESS

ForbesBooks

Published by ForbesBooks, Charleston, South Carolina.
Member of Advantage Media Group.

ForbesBooks is a registered trademark, and the ForbesBooks colophon is a trademark of Forbes Media, LLC.

Printed in the United States of America.

10 9 8 7 6 5 4 3 2 1

ISBN: 978-1-94663-353-8
LCCN: 2019906761

Book design by Carly Blake.

This publication is designed to provide accurate and authoritative information in regard to the subject matter covered. It is sold with the understanding that the publisher is not engaged in rendering legal, accounting, or other professional services. If legal advice or other expert assistance is required, the services of a competent professional person should be sought.

Advantage Media Group is proud to be a part of the Tree Neutral® program. Tree Neutral offsets the number of trees consumed in the production and printing of this book by taking proactive steps such as planting trees in direct proportion to the number of trees used to print books. To learn more about Tree Neutral, please visit **www.treeneutral.com**.

Since 1917, the Forbes mission has remained constant. Global Champions of Entrepreneurial Capitalism. ForbesBooks exists to further that aim by bringing the Stories, Passion, and Knowledge of top thought leaders to the forefront. ForbesBooks brings you The Best in Business. To be considered for publication, please visit **www. forbesbooks.com**.

This book is dedicated to my wife and best friend, Julie, along with my three beautiful daughters, Claudia, Payton, and Alison (Ali). Thanks to my dad, Frank, and my mom, Elaine, for raising me with solid values, an unbelievable work ethic, and the belief that I can accomplish anything. To my older sister, Michele, thanks for always supporting me.

TABLE OF CONTENTS

FOREWORD

"This is Mark," I said as I answered my cell phone one autumn Saturday morning in 2011. I generally do not answer calls on weekends. But, I did that morning. I'm glad I did.

"Mark, this is Shawn Burcham of Pro Food Systems in Holts Summit. Do you have a minute?"

Shawn is the founder and CEO of this amazing company now called PFSbrands. When he called me, Shawn had already guided his company well beyond the $20 million mark in sales along with landing on the Inc. 5000 list more than once. He wanted to know what an outsourced CFO could bring to the table.

I can now share the secret I've held since late 2011 regarding the value I brought to Shawn and his dedicated team—not much. I'm serious. All I did was make a few suggestions and gave Shawn a few reading assignments. Shawn and his team did the rest. Fast, that is. There is no such thing as first gear in this company.

My other secret is that I was able to get a good read on Shawn within about five minutes after meeting him in person. First, this highly likeable guy with a Hollywood, neighborly smile revealed two CEO traits I admire and appreciate: Shawn is decisive and he's humble. Oh, and one more thing: I quickly learned that his ideas machine is always in high gear on an Indianapolis speedway.

We simplified the financials, not to mention getting them rolled out earlier in the month. Shawn quickly took the lead in starting financial huddles with his management team. That led to identifying and tracking the most important metrics in the company. Playbook creation soon followed in sales, operations, and a new marketing department.

Shawn already had a rock-solid team, but as the company grew, continual upgrading along with applying the best practices of Top-grading became foundational puzzle pieces in attracting new team members who wanted to help this company soar even more so.

As each year passed, sales kept growing. More importantly, the stakeholders spoke too with their praise—customers, vendors, the entire PFSbrands family, and the community. Speaking of customers, I want to call out every wholesaler in the PFSbrands network from coast to coast—thank you for being important, strategic players in this growth.

Back to Shawn and the book you are about to read. The author is a husband, father, son, and brother. He's a great family man. The life of entrepreneurship is hard, lonely, and emotionally draining. Yet, I'm thankful for the family bond that has grown as the company has scaled, which comes with its own challenges, speed bumps, and unexpected detours along the way.

You'll also be reading about a CEO who drinks from the same cup he's sharing with you. Open-Book Management, building a great team, scaling, score keeping, all of it—his company is applying these practices daily. More importantly, his entire team is not content or complacent with their current success. They are continually raising the bar on these and other management practices Shawn will be sharing with you.

I'm also thankful that Shawn has included a chapter on ESOPs as PFSbrands is now employee-owned as of early 2017. ESOPs can be a complex, scary beast. Shawn has demystified the ESOP process and explained the steps toward employee ownership in terms we can all understand.

As you are reading the book, do not hesitate to ask for a LinkedIn connection with Shawn. Go ahead and shoot a question or two his way after he accepts your request. He'll answer those, too.

I'm thankful for the front row seat I've had since 2011 while watching this company grow in both sales and great people. But I've saved a seat for you right next to me. And I'm calling you a VIP. Enjoy the read. One more thing—let Shawn know the winning score in your business one year after you've read this book.

MARK GANDY

G3CFO, Free Agent CFO, CFO Bookshelf

INTRODUCTION
The Difference a Book Can Make

A lot of people ask me if I were shipwrecked and could only have one book, what would it be? I always say, How to Build a Boat.

STEPHEN WRIGHT

I had never been much of reader. I never read fiction books. I didn't read business books. I read all kinds of publications, newspapers, and other various types of articles related to my industry. Until I was forty years old, the only two books I had read in my entire life from cover to cover were *Where the Red Fern Grows* and *The Old Man and the Sea* way back in eighth grade. It's funny to think that I can even remember those books.

When my wife, Julie, and I started PFSbrands out of our home in 1998 (back then known as Pro Food Systems), I sure wasn't thinking about reading books, let alone writing them. Then one Saturday morning in late 2011, just before my forty-first birthday, I was in the office just as I spent nearly every Saturday, barring any family activities.

Our company had been transitioning, going through a massive growth cycle. I was buried in paperwork, working seventy to eighty hours per week. Top-line sales were fantastic, but PFSbrands was barely making any money. In fact, we had made the same amount of profit that year with $8 million more in revenue. Things didn't seem to be "clicking" internally. Something just wasn't right. In all honesty, looking back, I can see that things inside our company were really messed up.

That's when I decided to reach out to a part-time CFO by the name of Mark Gandy. I found his name while surfing the internet and discovered that he was located in nearby Columbia, Missouri. I was not necessarily fond of "consultants" at the time, but I picked up the phone and gave Mark a call, and he answered. *On a Saturday.*

Mark and I met later that next week and ended up establishing a working relationship. One of the best things Mark did for me was to encourage me to begin reading and studying. I resisted for a few weeks. I made all the usual excuses made by most business owners: "I'm too busy," "I don't have the time," "It won't help," "All the books are the same," etc. However, when he gave me a book entitled *The Danger Zone: Lost in Growth Transition,* by Jerry Mills, I read it from cover to cover in one night.

As I read the book, I felt like it was written about me. I could relate to so many of the challenges faced by entrepreneurs who were leading growing companies. The timing could not have been better because I realized I was in the danger zone and needed to get out. In the introductory letter, Jerry concluded by saying, "The goal of this book will have been accomplished if it helps one business owner avoid or escape the Danger Zone."

Thanks to Jerry's willingness to write *The Danger Zone* and his desire to help others, I am in a much better spot both personally and professionally as I write this.

Since reading that book, I've read hundreds more, and I can proudly say that I read and listen to dozens of new books each year. They are mostly business related, but I've read a few books for enjoyment, and numerous self-improvement books, including several on how to be a better husband and father. In fact, whenever I find myself in a situation where I need help, or if I need to improve in a certain area, or if I need to learn about something, I turn to books. I turn to the books written by those who are the most well-respected experts in their particular fields.

It's frustrating to think of what I may have missed in my first forty years without reading books. I wonder how much better I could be today if I had been a reader during those first forty years. Yet there's a quote on reading by Frank Serafini: "There is no such thing as a child who hates to read; there are only children who have not found the right book." You can replace "children" with "leader" or "CEO" and the same holds true.

That's what inspired me to write the *right* book.

Keeping Score with GRITT is in part intended to give our current and future wholesale customers, suppliers, franchisees, retailers, and employee -owners at PFSbrands a tool that allows them the opportunity to get to know my history, my beliefs, the history of PFSbrands, and the challenges that accompany business ownership. By sharing this information with each person who enters the company, I can ensure that everyone knows where we have been, and what the expectations are moving forward, and that every employee-owner at PFSbrands has the opportunity to excel in their personal and professional lives. By sharing this information with our customers and suppliers, my hope is that we can develop an even stronger partnership that allows all of us to become more successful within our extremely competitive business environment.

But this book is far bigger than PFSbrands. The ultimate purpose of this book is to help ANYONE become more successful in business and in life, to teach people about business and financial literacy, and to teach people how to *mentally* change in order to consistently improve as a person. Additionally, I want to

- inspire other entrepreneurs to start businesses and help them scale their businesses by creating a people-centric approach;

- encourage other business owners and business leaders to communicate more openly with their employees so that they can be more engaged at work;

- help people better themselves, focus on a positive attitude every day, set big goals, and become committed to learning every day and constantly improving;

- help leaders to become more self-aware of their strengths and weaknesses to enable them to become better servant leaders; and

- encourage business owners to consider ESOPs as a meaningful and legitimate business model.

This book is for the business owner, the CEO, the manager, or the employee who's just plain stuck and lacks the leadership or hope to pull out of the abyss they are currently in. Maybe your current reality is frustrating. You know you want to be more effective, have more fun, make more money, and have less stress. You know you want to be more successful. This book is for *you*, that one person who can never seem to get ahead. Whether you are an employee, a supervisor, a business owner, or even a CEO, being stuck in a rut is a lonely place to be.

This book likewise is for the business owner who is resistant to reading and studying, or the entrepreneur who thinks they are smarter than everyone else. The entrepreneur who believes nobody else under-stands what they are going through. This book is for the dedicated and results-driven employee —those hardworking individuals who feel like no one else gets it. For the entrepreneur who wants to scale up but doesn't know how to get there.

This book is for those leaders who want to establish a culture where employees are highly engaged, where those employees actually think and act like owners.

> This book is for those leaders who want to establish a culture where employees are highly engaged, where those employees actually think and act like owners.

Believe me, I've been there. I've failed a lot. But I never gave up. My failures became my raw material for future successes.

Anyone can win in the game of business and in the game of life. You need to dream big and believe that you can do anything you want. You need vision, a purpose, a goal, work ethic, a simple road map, and drive. You need a positive attitude every day, and you need to commit. Always surround yourself with people better than you who compensate for your weaknesses, challenge you, and hold you accountable. Find a way to write down your goals and KEEP SCORE with a great team around you. When you do these things, you have increased your odds of success. But even that's not enough.

You also need GRITT.

No, that's not a misspelling. GRITT is an acronym of key mind-sets—goal driven, responsible, involved, team, and tolerance of failure—and my tried-and-true business model (and life model) that delivers consistent results. It allows businesses to scale with success, while maintaining a people-centric approach. GRITT brought my business from a humble start-up in my garage to $60 million-plus and nineteen straight years of double-digit growth (and still going).

In *Keeping Score with GRITT: Straight Talk Strategies for Success*, you'll learn the fundamentals of strong rhythm, goal setting, and scaling processes, while exploring why moving to an Open-Book Management model and possibly even implementing an employee stock ownership plan (ESOP) can help bring your business to the next level.

Take it from someone who was never an avid reader: whatever you are facing, there is a lot to be learned from others who have experiences in the same area. One of my biggest regrets and mistakes in life is that I didn't start reading books until age forty. Reading has changed my life so much that I implemented a book club at PFSbrands to encourage and incentivize everyone to continue to grow and learn. I even require our senior leadership team to read a minimum of twelve books annually. I've seen dozens of people improve their lives as a result of implementing our book club. You can check out the simple book club application we use at www.betterbookclub.com.

The goal here is to make a BIG impact by helping others start THINKING BIG, by illustrating with some straight talk strategies for success how anyone can take more control over their work and their life. However, much like Jerry Mills stated in *The Danger Zone*, if this book helps just one person to make the personal changes necessary to become more successful in life, then I will consider it a tremendous success.

Now, I invite you to discover within this book how success for businesses and individuals comes down to *Keeping Score with GRITT*.

G R I T T

Goal-Driven **Responsible** **Involved** **Team** **Tolerance of Failure**

CORE PURPOSE

To help others become more successful in work and in life.

MISSION STATEMENT

We exist to empower our employee-owners and allow them the opportunity to build their futures by providing all of our customers with consistent, high-quality food products at reasonable prices and assisting our retail customers in operating profitable locations.

VISION STATEMENT

To be the best in customer service and innovation enabling us to establish five thousand branded food locations and become the leader in branded food service offerings within the market segments we compete in.

GUIDING PRINCIPLES

1. Satisfaction
Develop enthusiastically satisfied customers 100% of the time

2. High Standards
Apply the highest standard of excellence and hard work in all that we do

3. Improvement
Embrace a spirit of continuous improvement and constant expansion

4. Work Together
Consistently work as a TEAM and develop cohesiveness

5. Profitability
Recognize that profitability is essential to the success of our retailers and our employee-owners

CORE VALUES

Happiness Rule

Have fun

Always treat others as you want to be treated

Practice "ownership thinking"

Positive ATTITUDE always

I —There's no "I" in "TEAM"

No complaining

Entitlements do not exist

Structure and balance—God, family, work, and everything else

Straight talk and simple is better

Remember that the customer is why we are here

U never get a second chance to make a first impression

Learn to communicate openly through all channels

Everyone has the opportunity to excel

CHAPTER 1

Taking Flight: How Early Experiences Shaped a Pilot, Husband, and CEO

Clearly this was an out-of-the-ordinary landing,
but I was just doing my job and any one of our
pilots would have taken the same actions.

CAPTAIN DAVID WILLIAMS
(a pilot who landed a stricken jumbo jet without landing gear)

Flying an airplane is a lot like leading a successful organization. There are many moving parts involved, and every single one of your decisions determines whether you remain in the air and continue on a steady course toward your destination. In both instances, a lot can go wrong. You need to be able to make split-second decisions, trust in your training, and rely on that intangible gut feeling to make the right call at the right time. Because, at the end of the day, when you're in the air and you have the responsibility of others' lives depending on you, you have to be able to have that kind of innate confidence and decisiveness when the unexpected happens.

If those qualities are lacking in a leader, or in a pilot, it can cause all that momentum to tumble right out of the sky.

Models of the airplanes Shawn has owned.

The unexpected happened to me one day when I was flying a 1999 Bonanza A36 back from Kansas City following a short business trip. Of all things that could possibly happen, the door popped open midflight while we were cruising at seven thousand feet above the ground. I was flying by myself and had just received my instrument (IFR) rating, which was required by the insurance company prior to me being able to fly solo in this airplane. But, of course, a door popping open just happened to be the one thing that we didn't cover in flight school. What do you do when the door opens?

Well, at nearly two hundred miles per hour, it got really loud in the cabin. I couldn't shut the door because not only was it on the other side of the cabin, but the air pressure difference made it impossible to shut while in flight. With all the chaos and wind noise swirling around, I tried to remain calm and think. I knew where I was in proximity to the nearest airport, so I got on the radio and declared an emergency. The nearest airport happened to be Whiteman Air Force Base, and they began questioning me immediately. "November 55 Quebec Hotel, please verify that you are declaring an emergency and landing at Whiteman Airforce Base." I replied, "Affirmative, November 55 Quebec Hotel declaring an emergency and landing at Whiteman Airforce Base."

Already nervous enough, on final approach to landing I suddenly saw two fighter jets, one out each window, leveled off on both wings, escorting me down to the runway. That definitely wasn't covered in flight school, and needless to say was more than a little nerve racking. I had thoughts of cueing up the tower and saying: "Tower, this is Ghost Rider requesting a fly-by," but I thought my attempt at humor might not be well received. I was still a very new pilot

> **I suddenly saw two fighter jets, one out each window, leveled off on both wings, escorting me down to the runway.**

with just over eighty hours of total flight time. I had my instrument (IFR) rating, but at this time I had not flown a great deal by myself, because insurance companies require you to have certain ratings and flight time prior to flying alone. This was only my second solo flight in this airplane.

I managed to successfully get the plane down safely on a massive runway, a runway that is nearly three miles long and two hundred feet wide (after all, this is the home of the notorious B2 "stealth" bombers). The radio control tower instructed me to taxi my airplane all the way back to the end of the runway where I had just landed, park it, stay in the airplane, and wait for further instructions.

You can imagine—it is a huge feeling of relief with any in-air aviation incident if you make it to the ground and you live to tell about it. My heart was still racing but I was glad to be on the ground and glad that the airplane was not damaged in any way. Hell, I was glad the door hadn't flown off and taken out the rear stabilizer.

After what seemed like a long taxi back to the north end of the runway, and after I shut down the airplane, a gentleman who had flown General Aviation airplanes greeted me within minutes and informed me what was going to happen. He asked, "Have you served in any military branches?" I promptly replied, "No sir." He continued with, "Since I fly civilian airplanes, I just want to prepare you for what is going to take place. You're gonna have some guys show up in bomb suits, and they're gonna have their guns pointed at you. Be calm through that process and follow their instructions, because they are going to check your plane for bombs and find out why you are here." Calm? Yeah, right, got it.

My heart was already racing enough but now the blood pressure was really cranked up. I don't exactly remember how I replied but knowing me and my sense of humor it was probably something to the effect of "that sounds exciting."

Several men wearing big silver bomb suits showed up with rifles drawn, pointed right at me. They asked me who I was, what had happened, why I had landed here, and many other interrogation questions. After checking my plane for bombs, they asked me to get in one of their vehicles and they escorted me to an office. After I had been questioned by a couple different people for about two hours, they were satisfied that I was telling the truth: I was who I said I was, and I wasn't a threat. They escorted me back to my airplane, left sitting right where I parked it at the end of the runway, and they allowed me to leave. After looking the airplane over very well, and after making sure my door was shut, I took off for a quick fifteen-minute flight back home.

Thankfully, I was able to remain calm and navigate through the unexpected and land safely back at my home airport. Unbeknown to me, the Federal Aviation Administration, the governing body over all aviation activity, had already taken action over what occurred. They had informed my home base (the airport where each airplane owner registers their plane) and called my primary home number (obviously I was not there, since I was being interrogated for the past few hours). That meant that my prior flight instructor was waiting at the airport to ensure that I got back safely, and my wife was a nervous wreck wondering what in the heck had happened. I had turned my cell phone off earlier in the day before I took off for my flight and did not turn it back on until after getting home.

The NTSB is the governing body that investigates plane crashes. They report consistently that the majority of airplane accidents occur due to pilot error. I'd say the same comparison could be drawn for company failures. The majority of businesses fail due to leadership errors. There's a certain responsibility that comes with being in charge and taking on a leadership role. People are counting on you—your clients, your customers, your vendors, your employees, your family.

> People are counting on you—your clients, your customers, your vendors, your employees, your family.

Another pilot by the name of Ernest K. Gann once said, "Anyone can do the job when things are going right. In this [aviation] business we play for keeps." I believe the same can be said about business. When things are going right, leaders seem to be perceived as heroes. However, when things are not necessarily going as planned, the real leaders stand out.

Shawn's Cessna M2.

As the founder and CEO of PFSbrands, I'm constantly making critical decisions that keep our operation in the air and on target toward our goals. I know that at the end of the day my decisions are now affecting more than 130 different families and the loved ones of the employee-owners who work alongside me. My decisions affect the 1,500-plus locations promoting our brands—Champs Chicken, Cooper's Express, Private Label and BluTaco—from the state of Washington to the state of Florida as we move in our current trajectory toward over five thousand locations nationwide.

My decisions have helped guide us to $60 million-plus in revenue, nineteen years of double-digit growth, and nine years straight on the Inc. 5000 list as one of the fastest-growing privately held companies, something only .04 percent of the companies on the Inc. 5000 list have ever accomplished. These decisions have led to prestigious recognitions that are too numerous to mention in total, but include the Missouri Fast Track Award, the Great Game of Business All Star Award, and four straight years being recognized nationally as a Great Place to Work. Most importantly, my decisions have led to me being surrounded with exceptionally talented people, folks who embrace our core values wholeheartedly, and who are as driven as I am to constantly learn, adapt, and evolve. The highlights are nice, but you will find no complacency as we continue to move forward.

I'm also, thankfully, surrounded by people who like to Keep Score.

At our headquarters, we are surrounded by scoreboards—whiteboards and digital monitors all over the place with real-time data containing our key performance indicators (KPIs), such as the following:

- Total revenue

- Total branded accounts

- Gross margin

- Wages as percent to revenue

- Earnings before taxes (EBT)

- Earnings before interest, taxes, depreciation, and amortization (EBTIDA)

Regarding the last bullet point, many business owners or employees cannot tell you what EBITDA means. Our employee-owners can. Not only can they give you the definition, but they can also tell you how they are affecting and moving it in the right direction.

Some of those numbers can change daily, such as the total number of branded accounts. I can remember when they didn't change every day, moving at a snail's pace. Today, I'm proud to notice that total branded accounts are always moving. The entire company is focused on that number because it's part of our vision—to reach and exceed five thousand branded accounts. We put that vision in place at the end of 2011. That's one of our KPIs that people are in tune with, and our new branded accounts are what really drive our rapid growth.

As I walk through the office each day, I'm always looking at these "scoreboards." My hope is that everybody else is too. Even our

> Keeping score is a team effort, and that's what has driven our success.

customers and suppliers take notice, along with anybody else visiting our facility. Keeping score is a team effort, and that's what has driven our success. Well, that and GRITT, but we'll get to that later.

ORIGINS OF ENTREPRENEURSHIP

My office is filled with my passions. I've owned six different airplanes: a Bonanza A36, a TBM700, another Bonanza A36, a TBM850, a Cessna M2, and another TBM850. I have models of each of those airplanes on the top of my cabinets. I even have a real part from my M2 mounted on the wall, a nice $24,000 wingtip that was damaged after we hit a buzzard on final approach coming into North Carolina while taking some customers back from their trip to Missouri, where they had attended a PFSbrands Discovery Days event.

Regarding all the airplanes I've owned, people ask me which one I have enjoyed flying the most. The answer is "all of them." As a pilot, each time you step up to a larger, faster, more-complex airplane, there's a personal challenge involved in learning to fly it. As you move into turboprops and jets, there are more-stringent regulations involving the training you need to endure and the proficiency you need to demonstrate. However, after you complete these rigorous courses, you feel a massive sense of pride and accomplishment. In turbine aircraft, you are required to go through recurrent training every year in each plane. In my case, all of this training requires me to take time away from the business and clear my head so that I can focus on the important task of continuously improving my piloting skills. This involves a higher level of commitment and GRITT. I enjoy the challenge of flying and

I enjoy what aviation has done for my businesses and my family.

And then there's my love for books. I have them all over the place in my office, and lots of pictures adorning the walls. These include pictures of my family and one of my favorite motivational pictures that I've had my entire professional career from before I graduated college. It shows a picture of a baseball player successfully sliding headfirst into second base and reads: "Opportunity always involves some risk. You can't steal second base and keep your foot on first."

I can remember my dad teaching me a life lesson at about the age of seven. Before one of my first baseball practices, he said something like, "If you want to be successful at whatever you decide to do, show up earlier than everyone else, work harder and smarter than everyone else, and stay later than everybody else." Obviously, his message was that you don't necessarily have to be more talented than others, you just have to outwork, outhustle, and outsmart them.

The work ethic needed to succeed, and my entrepreneurial spirit, were instilled in me at an early age. I grew up in Farmington, Missouri, which is a small town in the southeastern part of the state. Farmington is located between St. Louis and what most people refer to as the "bootheel of Missouri," so I guess that's where my speaking accent came from. My older sister and I were fortunate to be raised by two loving parents with a strong faithful and moral code. I was also fortunate to know one of my grandfathers and both grandmothers. Looking back, it's pretty obvious how my parents developed the strong core values that helped to shape their lives and the lives of my sister and me. Those values came from their parents and continued to get passed down to us. Not everyone has the benefit of that kind of family unit, so it's always been important to me in a business environment to establish the proper expectations through a set of core values.

While video games were beginning to take shape during my

childhood, I preferred to be outside whenever possible, whether it was scaling dirt piles, climbing trees, riding go-karts or three-wheelers, or playing whiffle ball or baseball or basketball or football—I just loved it, especially if it involved competition. As I got old enough to venture away from the house and into the neighborhood, the main rule was to be home at dinnertime. Those of you who grew up in a small town, in an old-fashioned rural environment, you know what I am talking about.

I settled into basketball and baseball as I got into competitive sports, though baseball was my real passion. I would spend hours throwing the tennis ball or racquetball against a wall and pretending I was Ozzie Smith or Tommy Herr.

I was raised by a "stay-at-home mom." Those of you who are "stay-at-home moms" know why I put this phrase and its implication of "just being home" in quotations. Mom was, and still is, an extremely hardworking woman, and she had a tremendous influence on my upbringing. Her father was a dragline operator on the Missouri River, but he was a very good businessman as well, ultimately purchasing numerous farms on or near the river bottom.

There is no doubt that his business acumen rubbed off on Mom. When conducting business, she could get to the point quickly and didn't make a lot of small talk. She's a very tough lady and always expected a lot out of my sister and me. Looking back, I realize that her work ethic was absolutely amazing. However, she always put God and family above everything else.

My father spent the majority of his career in the childcare industry. He worked his own way through an undergraduate degree, then continued on to earn and pay for his master's degree. To this day I'm amazed at how Dad knows a little bit about everything. He's always been a real hero and mentor to me, though we don't talk about him that way. He would be the last person to take credit for something like that. But he's an incredible example of someone who truly cares about others. His professional career was centered around helping abused and neglected children. Later in life, he and Mom owned a residential care facility where they cared for veterans. Throughout Dad's life, he has ALWAYS put others' needs before his own. He's dedicated his life to helping others.

Despite it all, Dad spent a lot of time in the front yard hitting me ground balls on the choppy terrain. I can't even venture to guess how many balls he served up over the years. Looking back now, I don't know how he did it. After a full day of work, from his main job to working on side projects to make an extra buck, he rarely turned me down for a request to hit some grounders. I'd venture to say that not too many fathers who worked as hard as he did took that amount of time to spend with their kids. However, even with all of the "fun stuff," many of my best memories of spending time with my father revolved around work.

At a very young age, my father taught me how to mow grass, both with a push mower and a riding mower. By the age of eight I was mowing by myself on the riding lawn mower, sitting on the front edge of the seat just so I could reach the pedals. I don't ever remember feeling overwhelmed by having to do work around the house. Work was just a part of life, as far as I knew. And Dad always had a project he wanted help with. As I got older, it was I who needed help with projects. Things like putting a new stereo in my car or even a new engine. Most people don't know it, but Dad and I framed out the offices and constructed the original walk-in coolers and freezers at the first PFSbrands building.

The thing I didn't know until I got older was how many life lessons and core values I learned from my dad while we were working. He was notorious for slipping in advice without me realizing that he was teaching.

Then at age fourteen I took my drive, goals, and a few bucks and started my own lawn care business with my childhood best friend. Yep, business owner at age fourteen. We had business cards and went door to door to sell our services, and I drove a riding lawn mower and trailer full of push mowers and Weed eaters all over town, with no driver's license. I made good money mowing lawns for a couple of summers, especially for a teenage kid.

During my high school years, I continued to play basketball, but most of my spare time was spent playing and practicing baseball. I played on our high school baseball team, and then in the summers I played on one or two other teams. All the practice paid off and I learned a lot about team comradery through trips to Colorado with an all-star team and trips to state playoffs with a high school team.

After graduating from high school, I decided to drop the baseball aspirations and attend Southwest Missouri State University (now Missouri State University). I had no idea what I was going to major in, but I wanted to move on with my life. At the time, I was simply ready to get away from home and develop my independence.

The best thing that happened to me in college was meeting Julie in the middle of my sophomore year. One of her sorority sisters, whom I knew well set the two of us up on a blind date for their winter sorority dance.

I definitely was not looking for a serious girlfriend at the time. I was having a lot of fun, and that reflected in my first semester sophomore grades. I was also feeling comfortable in my second year of college and fraternity life. I found a way to stay competitive in a team sport by helping our fraternity to win several intramural softball championships. The fraternity provided some leadership opportunities, but I still had not declared a major and wasn't sure what I wanted to study. Life was good though and Julie was somehow different than any other girl I had dated. I just couldn't spend enough time with her and we were becoming best friends.

We had a lot of similarities. She was from a small town called Auxvasse, ironically located in the same county where my mom and dad had met nearly twenty-five years earlier. Auxvasse was (and is) a town of only nine hundred people. Like me, Julie also grew up with a stay-at-home mom and an older sibling, although her older sibling was a brother. Everything between us seemed to be coincidental, including the fact that our values and work ethic were perfectly aligned.

Her father, Roger, was and still is in the grocery business. Very much an entrepreneur himself, he started at the age of sixteen washing windshields at the gas station that he ended up leasing at age nineteen, later purchasing the station. Roger and I have always gotten along great over the years, I think in large part because of our work ethic and a mutual interest in business. From what I've been told, he always liked to try to intimidate Julie's boyfriends, including me. He'd give me that intimidating stare and call me "boy," because I was dating his daughter. "Boy" was fairly common in the Moser household and that became evident as I later met all of Julie's uncles. One of Roger's favorite questions was: "Boy, you got a job?" I always had the right answer.

Having grown up in an entrepreneurial family, Julie was all primed for entrepreneurial life—primed or cursed, however you want to look at it. Things have changed a lot since that first date in January 1991, and Julie has been there to support me and see us through all of these changes.

Just before my college graduation, while we were attending my last fraternity White Rose formal, I asked her to marry me. She said yes, and then she took the next year to finish her business education degree. We got married two weeks after her college graduation in 1994.

Looking back, I'm sure our parents were questioning the timing, probably even the legitimacy. But guess what? That's just how we roll! As you'll learn, we've spent the last twenty-seven years taking chances together, not often worrying about what others think, and doing things that at times don't seem to make sense. Julie has always had confidence in me. She's always been supportive and understanding with the risks that accompany business ownership. If you are familiar with the Kolbe score, I'm the definition of a "quick start" personality type. I'm decisive and make decisions quickly, oftentimes just based on my gut instinct. Julie takes a little more time and has a more analytical and cautious approach. This has provided a good balance and, as you can imagine, some frustration over the years. Despite what she may tell you, I always appreciate her opinion.

THE BUSINESS OF CHEESE

During my junior year in college, I applied for an internship at Mid-America Farms. Mid-America Farms was the "marketing arm" of Mid-America Dairymen, one of the largest dairy cooperatives in the country at the time, and growing rapidly. Today, they're known as Dairy Farmers of America.

Tom Goddard interviewed me. He was the leader of the Packaged and Processed Cheese Division at Mid-America Farms. I don't really remember a lot about the interview with Tom Goddard other than one question. He asked, "Why did you choose SMSU as your college?"

I answered, "Because I had heard the girl-to-guy ratio was seven to one."

Honestly, I thought I had blown the interview. I'm not even sure that statistic was correct. But I guess Tom thought I was honest because somehow, I got offered the internship. I later learned that Tom had a great sense of humor, so maybe that's why he decided to take a chance on me. I didn't know this at the time, but I was the first intern in the "sales area" for Mid-America Farms. I was actually paving the way for their internship program. I reported to a fantastic woman by the name of Diane Westbrook. Diane had worked with Tom for many years and I'm thankful for her guidance at the time.

Mid-America Dairymen was a high-growth company with a well-respected CEO, and I was gaining valuable real-world business experience. Furthermore, I was working for a cooperative owned by dairy farmers, an experience that would benefit me later in life. For those of you who are unfamiliar with what that is, a "cooperative" is a company that is owned by its customers. The sole purpose of Mid-America Dairymen was to purchase ALL of the milk a dairy farmer could produce and provide that farmer the highest possible price for the milk. The mentality within a cooperative is all about "helping others to be more successful." I could not have asked for a better start to my career.

> The mentality within a cooperative is all about "helping others to be more successful." I could not have asked for a better start to my career.

After graduating college, I was selected to "pilot" a new sales training program for Mid-America Farms. I had successfully piloted the first intern program, so they created another program for me to lead. I have to thank Tom Goddard for pushing upper management to create this new training position. Mid-America Farms gave me the opportunity to work in customer service, purchasing, logistics, accounting, operations, human resources, and, of course, sales.

After about twelve months of the training program, someone resigned, and I stepped into the role of regional sales manager for the Packaged and Processed Cheese Division, working under my mentor Tom Goddard and alongside my mentor Diane Westbrook.

I credit Tom for the first core value of PFSbrands, which is HAVE FUN. Tom was a great storyteller, loved to tell jokes, and had a great personality. He had an incredible work ethic, but he was always joking around and having a good time. On all of his presentations and on his annual plans, he would always start with encouraging everyone to HAVE FUN. His philosophy was a little out of the box in the corporate "suit and tie" world, and the dairy cooperative environment wasn't exactly centered around fun. But I picked up a lot of tremendous leadership skills from Tom during my years at Mid-Am.

My career there involved a lot of travel. I traveled across the entire country and was in and out of airplanes, rental cars, and motels Monday through Thursday. It was a great experience. While there, I began to develop a love for selling and building relationships. Even with selling an item like cheese, my approach was always centered around finding ways to add value and help someone become more successful. I could help them sell more product, lower portion costs, provide a product that melted faster or slower, or possibly provide a different size or type of shredded cheese. I never knew there was so much to know about cheese. I worked to become extremely knowledgeable in my field. At the young age of twenty-five, I was far from an expert, but I worked hard to understand the business, know my cheese facts, set goals, and develop my professional skills.

EMERGING FROM DISCONTENT

Leaving Mid-America Dairymen in 1996 was an extremely difficult decision. I really liked the people there and they had been extremely good to me. I could see a good career path ahead. I was becoming better at what I did every day. But the progression to grow profession-ally at Mid-Am would require a lot of overnight travel, and with Julie and me talking about having our first child, I simply did not want to be gone overnight that much.

My father-in-law, Roger, who owned several supermarkets in central Missouri, was a customer of Hays Food Systems based out of St. Peters. They were an authorized distributor for Chester Fried Chicken, which was a branded chicken program primarily targeting convenience stores but also selling to supermarkets. Roger had four Chester Fried locations with Hays, and happened to be good friends with the owner. After an introduction and an interview, I ended up accepting a regional sales manager position with Hays. Suddenly I had gone from a large Fortune 500 company to a small business environment. This was a major change, but a great opportunity for me to continue learning.

While working for Hays Food Systems, I managed western Missouri and all of Kansas. I immediately inherited two individuals to manage, so this position provided me my first opportunity to lead others. I was primarily responsible for selling and opening new Chester Fried locations inside convenience stores and supermarkets. During that time, I got some real-world small business experience, and quickly learned something very important—I was simply not cut out to work for other people. I often look back and wonder what would have happened if I had had the opportunity to work for an outstanding business owner who truly cared about others. What if I had had the opportunity to work for a company that spent a lot of time on their culture and the leadership team sincerely wanted to help others become successful? In my case, I doubt it would have made a difference, because I had an entrepreneurial drive inside me that was pushing me to do something on my own. With that being said, I've come to realize over the years that people generally don't leave jobs because of the business; people most often leave because of their bosses.

> I've come to realize over the years that people generally don't leave jobs because of the business; people most often leave because of their bosses.

I was raised in an environment where I was taught "If you can't say something nice about someone, don't say anything at all." My father used to tell me, "Don't cut someone else off at the knees to make yourself look taller." I've carried this message through life and make it a point to never talk badly about a competitor. I say all of this only to clarify that the person I worked for at Hays Food Systems was not in any way a bad person. In fact, I learned a lot from him. Our core values were simply not aligned, and that made for a difficult work environment for me. In the end, this work experience helped to mold me into the leader I am today.

After a while of working at Hays Food Systems, I was diligently pursuing something that would allow me to work for myself. Eventually, I ran across an advertisement that seemed interesting and potentially lucrative, and in the end Pro Food Systems became officially incorporated on July 13, 1998, with the purchase of some automated cappuccino machines with built-in drink counters. I placed these machines in local restaurants, went in every other weekend to replenish the supplies, and charged the operators for each drink that was produced.

Ultimately, I ended up with a total of sixteen machines and I made a little bit of extra income to supplement the pay from my real job. However, it was evident that the cappuccino business was not going to provide a solid source of income for my family. The volume of drinks that we were selling through the machines simply wasn't very large. This was due in part to the restaurants not necessarily recommending the drinks. On the other hand, I wasn't and still am not a coffee drinker, so this could have caused me to not be overly passionate about the business.

I continued to scour entrepreneur magazines and explore businesses for sale hoping to find the "perfect" opportunity. I was getting desperate to get out of the toxic small business environment I was in and find something more satisfying that I could devote my energy to.

During this time of professional discontent while working for Hays Food Systems, I noticed our primary supplier, Chester Fried Chicken, beginning to make several … *changes*. I was nervous about how these changes may affect my current employer, since his entire business model depended on his relationship with the company that controlled the Chester Fried name. I was growing increasingly uncertain of the direction they were headed in, and soon began to see some financial red flags with my current employer. Knowing today what I know about cash flow, I understand the situation even better now than I did at the time. I was working for an owner who had a great product and was a good salesman, but he wasn't necessarily managing the growth of the business, or the cash flow. This isn't uncommon for small business owners and today I see it all the time. Granted, at the time I was mostly naive about running a business and I thought that I knew more than I actually did. However, with the changes happening at Chester Fried corporate and with the misaligned core values at Hays Food Systems, I felt it was necessary for me to find something different so I could directly bring about my own success.

That's when I caught my break. I connected with BKI, a food-service equipment-manufacturing company based in South Carolina. BKI made one of the best automatic-lift deep fryers and deli hot cases on the market. I reached out to them in hopes that they might sell equipment to PFSbrands so that we could start our own branded chicken program. In the late 1990s, companies such as BKI established what they called "exclusive" distributors across the country. This meant that I would have to convince them that I could sell products for them, meet specified quotas, provide installation training on the equipment, and provide service on the equipment after the installation. No problem for someone who loves the pressure associated with producing results! In return for my commitment to perform, BKI would offer me a "protected" area where others could not sell BKI products.

Looking back, I realize how much of a stretch this was for BKI to award a territory to someone who didn't even sell food-service equipment. All I had to offer BKI was my *idea and vision* to create a new branded chicken program. As a publicly traded company, BKI wasn't interested in the chicken business, they were simply interested in selling more food-service equipment.

However, one winter day a BKI representative by the name of John Voegeli met me in Rolla, Missouri, to discuss the opportunity. John was fairly new at BKI, but he had come from a company called Broaster Company (Broaster). Broaster was recognized, much like Chester Fried, for using a branded chicken program to create breading and equipment sales to supermarket and convenience store owners. John was about my age, and because of his Broaster background, he believed in the power of a brand to drive these equipment sales.

I just needed to show him that I had some locations ready to get on board and convince him that I could launch a new brand that ultimately would drive equipment sales for BKI.

STEP UP TO THE PLATE
Turning Ideas into Action

Every experience we have in life, both the good and the bad, shapes who we are. Some of those experiences are expected and help us along our individual journeys to become successful, like schooling, work, and solid relationships with others. Yet it is in the unexpected experiences where we sometimes learn the most about life ... and about ourselves. I never would have known I could handle a midflight issue as a pilot had I not been faced with it. And that experience has given me a sense of peace and confidence even to this day that I can handle any problem that may arise while flying. The same holds true for the discontent I felt while working for Hays Food Systems. If that hadn't happened, I might not have decided to strike out on my own.

1.	Do you have a door that has unexpectedly opened in your business? What are you doing about it?

2.	Do you use any type of score keeping system in your business? If not, why not? If you do, what are the five to seven most important numbers you think you should track?

3.	How has your past shaped your life today? How are you now shaping the lives of those you lead or influence?

4.	Write down two or three key actions you will start today based on what you learned in this chapter.

CHAPTER 2

Humble Beginnings: The Origin Story of PFSbrands

We're not in the food business serving people.
We're in the people business serving food.

SHAWN BURCHAM

You have to know my father-in-law to know that conversations with him aren't very long. This was especially true twenty-five years ago, but it's just always been his style. Conversations are usually short and to the point. I think that's why we've gotten along so well over the years, because we can have a direct conversation, not really say much, and we're good.

Julie and I were still living in southwest Missouri, but we had driven up to her parents' house for the weekend in early 1999. The four of us were on our way to a restaurant called Sir Winston's in Fulton. There were not a lot of restaurant choices in the area at that time, so Sir Winston's was a common place for us to eat. Roger was driving us in his Lincoln Town Car, with him and my mother-in-law in the front, and Julie and me riding in the back.

Julie and I had already made the decision that we were going to go full steam ahead with PFSbrands, and I needed to give my resignation pretty soon because we were getting to the point where our next steps couldn't be done ethically, since we were getting ready to create a company in direct competition with my current employer. We were going to need to begin working on key suppliers and we wanted to ensure that there were no conflicts of interest with my current employer.

From the back seat, I told Roger what we were doing, that we were getting ready to go into business for ourselves, striking out on our own. I told him I was really close to signing an exclusive distributorship deal with BKI, a reputable equipment company based out of South Carolina. I told him that Julie and I were going to create a chicken program of our own—Champs Chicken, with the brand revolving around a racing theme. At the time, Julie and I were huge racing fans and rarely missed a NASCAR event on TV each weekend. Roger was a race car driver himself and had been racing pro-modified cars on dirt for the previous ten-plus years. He had recently purchased a car built to run on pavement that he raced in some NASCAR Goodies Dash Series events, at places like the Daytona and Charlotte Speedways. I knew the Champs Chicken racing theme would appeal to him since he was a fan as well.

But, remember, Roger had been a customer of Hays Food Systems for many years. He had Chester Fried Chicken programs in four of his stores. Roger and my boss at the time not only had a supplier/customer relationship, but they were also friends, which was ultimately how I secured my job at Hays Food Systems. Roger, much like me, has traditionally been very loyal to his suppliers, so I knew this was going to put him in a difficult situation.

With everything on the line, I just laid it out there and said I was curious if he might be interested in converting his stores over to our new program. We're talking about a huge leap, basically giving up a well-known chicken program and helping to pioneer a new one.

He was silent for a moment or two. Then he said, "Well, I guess if you do it, I'll go with you."

So in the backseat of my father-in-law's Town Car, I received my first big win, with four committed Champs Chicken locations under my belt. With a lot of work yet to do, a couple of weeks later I finalized my deal with BKI and I had an exclusive territory of my own.

> In the backseat of my father-in-law's town car, I received my first big win, with four committed Champs Chicken locations under my belt.

BKI had decided to take a chance on PFSbrands. They offered me an hourglass-shaped territory in Missouri that excluded St. Louis and Kansas City, but encompassed Springfield (the third largest city in the state). The new territory BKI carved out consisted mostly of rural areas that would not appeal to most equipment companies. But it was perfect for me to begin marketing a new branded chicken program. The contract was highly favored toward BKI and I really didn't have any assurance that I could keep the BKI territory. I even had to pay BKI on COD credit terms, which was understandable since PFSbrands did not have any type of solid credit history. However, BKI gave me an opportunity, and that was all I needed. After visiting several banks to secure a $75,000 working capital loan through an SBA program, I was ready to be an entrepreneur.

After leaving my full-time job in March 1999 and over the following seven years, PFSbrands grew our BKI hourglass-shaped territory in

Missouri to an exclusive territory that touched eight states around Missouri. We had become one of BKI's best distributors, growing our BKI sales every single year. After the recession hit in 2008, BKI was searching for ways to capture more revenue, so they began to deviate from most of their exclusive contracts in favor of selling to numerous food-service dealers. For several years, PFSbrands was the largest distributor for BKI and we still remain one of their top customers.

CHAMPS CHICKEN

In early March 1999, I was close to having all of the pieces put together to establish Champs Chicken. I was diligent about ensuring that I did not do anything unethical to compete with my current employer. Although I didn't have any type of signed noncompete agreement, I was aware of the fact that this venture was going to be in conflict with my current employer. To complicate things even more, I had hired my best friend, Brad, to work with me at Hays Food Systems more than a year earlier. I knew his future would be in jeopardy after I announced this resignation to my employer.

The stress of knowing that I was going to be competing with my current employer was almost overwhelming. Furthermore, I was continuing to sell new deals for a company that was shortly going to become my competitor. Therefore, two days after selling my last Chester Fried account, just before spring of 1999, I decided to turn in my resignation at Hays Food Systems. In addition, Brad ended up joining me in the launch of Champs Chicken. Needless to say, this was not well received by Hays. However, I had made a decision to move forward with my own business. I had not set out to create a competing business model, but I fell into a once-in-a-lifetime opportunity with BKI and I was excited to finally become my own boss. At the age of twenty-seven,

I thought I could create a better business model by having the right equipment and a solid branded chicken program.

The first few weeks involved finalizing some important product needs. I was facing the harsh reality of being a new business. I was searching for suppliers and had no history to show these folks that I was capable of paying for their goods. Most suppliers, including BKI, had me on COD terms. Fortunately, I was able to convince a few, including my largest one, which was my breading supplier, to extend some credit terms to me.

I'm indebted to Steve Holtsclaw, who has been a valuable breading supplier since day one. Steve is a small businessman too. In nearly twenty years of doing business together, he has never asked for a financial statement. He has also been one of our most dedicated and committed suppliers year after year. In that first year, his help was instrumental as we navigated a minor problem when we were getting ready to roll out our first location—we still didn't have our breading formula completely finalized.

We were trying to get our recipe nailed down, so there was a lot of test cooking going on in Texas and Missouri. In the food industry, when you are trying to match products, it's crucial during a transition to try one product against the other. To make sure that we had our breading and batter mix formulas nailed down, we tested and changed our formula dozens of times, so that the consumers would be satisfied with the new recipe.

We didn't have a test kitchen back then, so imagine being in a local supermarket deli, standing there cooking in the fryer, and as the chicken comes out, you're tasting the original product and comparing to your new product. Is it any good? Are they different? The same? What can be tweaked to make it just as good, if not better? How does the color compare? How about the crispiness? How does the product hold up in the hot case? Now imagine doing all this and trying to stay out of the way while the deli staff works to prepare products for their normal customers.

During this formulation process, I had Steve blending various breading formulations at his factory down in Texas, and he was sending me multiple different samples. We'd mail him a base sample to go off of, and he'd get to work reformulating it—reverse engineering it, if you will. It's actually a little more of an art than you might think. It's not simple to reproduce a product when you're trying to get the color and a crispiness match that customers are used to. We also wanted to make the product *better* than our competitors, which complicated things even more. I'm sure we went through more than twenty different formulations trying to get it right.

The other hurdle we had in starting a new branded chicken program was the boxes. I had no idea boxes could be so complicated. I thought that would be the easy part, but to get a customized, pre-printed chicken box takes an order of massive volume. For our first Champs Chicken location, I was only able to source plain white boxes. Even these plain white boxes were extremely difficult to find, since most boxes contained some type of graphics. However, we found some plain white boxes and were able to buy some stick-on labels that contained the Champs Chicken logo. Julie and I sat at our kitchen table unpacking ten thousand white boxes, putting a label on each box, and then repacking the boxes in the master case.

As we prepared to go forward and open our first stores, I knew my father-in-law was going backward with his image. He was converting from a recognized Chester Fried Chicken box to a plain white box with a label slapped on it. In addition to this, we had a slightly different breading formula, so these changes were definitely going to be noticed by the consumers.

Shawn applying labels on boxes for the first store opening in 1999.

OUR FIRST STORE AND KEEPING SCORE

Company history was made on a mild, sunny day, April 30, 1999, when we opened our first Champs Chicken account in Auxvasse, Missouri. As of this writing, this Champs Chicken location is still open. The convenience store was, and still is, owned by Show Me Oil Company, Inc. Incidentally, my in-laws, Roger and Jeanie Moser, are the sole shareholders of Show Me Oil Company, which started more than fifty years ago. I owe them a big thanks for taking a chance on a new chicken brand to replace the proven Chester Fried brand that they had in their store prior to converting over to Champs Chicken. While we feel our brand is superior today, it certainly wasn't back in 1999.

The years from 1999 to 2011 went by incredibly fast. I worked countless hours in and on the business, constantly trying to figure things out as I went along.

The early years were really tough. I had a lot to learn as a new business owner. I didn't always handle the stress well, at home or at work. Brad resigned early on because there just wasn't enough cash flow to support both of us. I ended up hiring him back a year later after I thought the business was at a point where I could "put him in the right seat." The business quickly got to the point where it needed more growth and I needed people on the team who were able to drive the top-line revenue. Brad was living three hours away and his contribution to the company was in more of a support role versus a driver role. Because of these things, I felt he wasn't the right fit for what we needed at the time.

I blame myself for the position I had put both of us in. However, I didn't communicate very well in those early days, because I was under the false impression that everyone knew what was going on in our business. Our lifelong friendship ended because I didn't handle things appropriately. While a change undoubtedly needed to occur, and I know I did the right thing for the survival of the business, I wish I knew then what I know today. I wish I could have this situation back for a redo. On the golf course, I'd beg for a mulligan. Today, given all the difficult conversations I've navigated, and given all of the research I've done on crucial conversations, I'm confident I would handle this conversation far better. This is the dark side of business ownership. Only entrepreneurs who have lived through this type business/friendship challenge can relate to it.

Growth was significant, cash was always a challenge, and profits seemed to be almost nonexistent. From 2008 to 2011, we grew our top-line sales by more than $12 million and more than doubled the size of the company. However, our bottom line reflected virtually no improvement. To top it all off, we were in the middle of a recession and my primary lending institution, like many other banks, was in major financial trouble due to loan defaults.

What seemed to be easy access to growth capital prior to 2008 was now a major concern that was threatening to cripple PFSbrands. I realized that I needed some CFO help, but I couldn't see a way to justify the expense. I had heard about part-time CFOs, so I began searching the internet. Yet I was extremely hesitant because I figured that I would get the typical "consultant" wanting to charge by the hour and provide useless knowledge that would turn out to be far from what I needed. I was not a fan of consultants at that time.

Fortunately, the first email I sent was to Mark Gandy, and he ended up being the only part-time CFO that I interviewed. Mark has been, and continues to be, a valuable resource. Late in 2011, he recommended several books for me to read. One of those books was *The Great Game of Business*, by Jack Stack. After reading the book, I realized as an entrepreneur I was already practicing several of the strategies mentioned. Since I had an athletic background, I had routinely referred to our business as a game and I thought of myself as a coach. I was actually playing a game, or at least partially.

The problem was, I didn't fully realize that I was participating in a game. Even worse, I wasn't Keeping Score, and I didn't realize that I could do far more as our head coach to get all of my players involved and get them Keeping Score as well.

> I didn't fully realize that I was participating in a game. Even worse, I wasn't keeping score.

I've never been one to rely on advice from just ONE person. Because of this, I was still a bit of a skeptic about reading, because I didn't feel that any one book could provide the answers. I was right. It actually took numerous books and a spirit of continuous learning.

Through reading, I was really picking up a lot of knowledge. So I continued reading more books.

These books would ultimately shape the vision I had for PFSbrands. After reading *Good to Great,* by Jim Collins; *Mastering the Rockefeller Habits,* by Verne Harnish; *Ownership-Thinking,* by Brad Hams; *The No Complaining Rule,* by Jon Gordon; and *Simple Numbers, Straight Talk, Big Profits,* by Greg Crabtree, I was on my way to a far better path for PFSbrands. I continued to immerse myself in business and leadership books, taking useful action items from each and every one of them. The books that have helped shape PFSbrands are far too many to mention.

Not only did I realize that I was in a game, but I actually had a game plan. Up until then, we had the following mission statement at PFSbrands: to provide all of our customers with consistent, high-quality food products at reasonable prices, and assist our retail customers in operating profitable locations.

CREATING CLARITY TO NAVIGATE THE GROWING PAINS

As PFSbrands grew from 1998 to 2011, you can imagine that my role changed significantly as a leader. I was still highly involved in the day-to-day business in 2011, but my mind-set had changed significantly. When I left my full-time employment in 1999, what started out as an opportunity to be my own boss quickly turned into a critical role of family provider. The reality of NO INCOME quickly set in, and I was now solely responsible for my wife of five years and a newborn baby daughter that was almost one year

> We instantly went from a double-income family with no kids, to a NO-INCOME family with one kid.

old. To put things into perspective and explain the risk that Julie and I took on, I always like to say it this way: "We instantly went from a double-income family with no kids, to a NO-INCOME family with one kid." There was no "security net" in 1999; the pressure was on me to make this business work.

After reading numerous books at the end of 2011, I had a life-changing revelation. I realized that what really "made me tick" as a human being was helping other people. Maybe a hereditary trait passed down from my father? Regardless of the reasoning, I had found my personal "why" in life. Up until this time, I had always enjoyed helping my customers become more successful, but my role was changing within my business. I was spending a lot of time in the office versus the time I had previously spent in front of my customers. Whether I wanted to or not, there were just too many things that needed to be done at the office, and this included hiring new people to keep up with the demands of our business.

What I realized was that I enjoyed creating opportunities and helping people get better. I enjoyed the coaching aspect of leadership, whether on or off the field. I realized that PFSbrands needed a bigger reason for WHY we existed. We were far more than a chicken company—I just had not communicated this effectively to our team.

In his book *Start with Why*, Simon Sinek details the importance of creating a company where the WHY is bigger than the WHAT. I had not read Simon's book in 2011, but I realized that our mission statement needed to really explain why PFSbrands was doing what we do. Yet, as I reflected on this, I didn't want to completely recreate our mission statement. I felt that it clearly laid out things that were important to me as a founder. I ended up adding fifteen words to the start of our mission statement, so it now read:

We exist to empower our employees and allow them the opportunity to build their futures by providing all of our customers with consistent, high-quality food products at reasonable prices and assisting our retail customers in operating profitable locations.

Knowing what I know today, I'm sure there will be critics out there who say our mission statement is too long. However, every word in this mission statement is important. If you're on the critic side and you think our mission statement is too long, just use the first fifteen words because those are the most important.

Let's dig into the mission statement a little deeper.

The words "We exist" clearly explain what a mission statement is. A mission statement is supposed to describe *why* your company exists. "To empower our employees" states that we are a company that wants employees to make decisions. The next portion, "and allow them the opportunity to build their futures," indicates that every employee that comes into this company has an OPPORTUNITY to build their future. We are not an entitlement-based company, and we will give 110 percent to every single employee. However, we do have high expectations and

> We expect our employees to EARN their rewards by dedicating themselves to consistent improvement.

we expect our employees to EARN their rewards by dedicating themselves to consistent improvement.

Our mission statement goes on to read: "by providing all of our customers with consistent, high-quality food products at reasonable prices …" Our customers include wholesalers, retailers, and consumers, which provides challenges to ensure that we are taking care of each segment. Our mission is to provide consistency and high quality. We feel strongly that we can do this with reasonable prices, but we do not strive to have the cheapest prices.

The mission statement closes with, "and assisting our retail customers in operating profitable locations." It is extremely important that we provide the necessary support to our retail customers to help them become more profitable.

If we didn't do this, we would not have the strong business model that exists today.

STEP UP TO THE PLATE
Turning Ideas into Action

Much like Southwest Airlines is open about the fact that they put their employees first, I realized in 2011 that I had historically done the same thing because of my own core values and beliefs. When people would ask me how I'd been able to grow PFSbrands so consistently over time, I always replied with, "We have awesome people." This new mission statement now indicated to everyone that PFSbrands is committed to helping our employees to build their futures. By taking care of our employees first, we believe that our employees will be better prepared and far more motivated to take care of our customers.

Questions to consider:

1. What challenges have you faced in your career and what did you do to overcome them?

2. What is your core purpose and mission statement for the company you lead or work for?

3. What's your personal core purpose? What makes you feel satisfied?

4. Who helped you to get where you are today?

5. Who can you thank today that has taken a risk to allow you an opportunity to have employment?

CHAPTER 3

The Happiness Rule: Thirteen Core Values for Lifelong Success

---

*Life is 10 percent what happens to you
and 90 percent how you respond to it.*

LOU HOLTZ

A s a young business owner, I was unaware that a company needed core values to hang their hat on. Then again, in a small company, every customer, vendor, and employee can see how the owner lives and behaves. Accordingly, employees tend to naturally behave as the owner does. That's not so true when the business grows. Documenting, teaching, and overcommunicating core values become new priorities as the business becomes more complex as the company grows. If you don't do these things, then you can expect chaos.

The core values of our organization are those values we hold that form the foundation on which we perform work and conduct ourselves. We have an entire universe of values, but some of them are so primary and so important to us that throughout the changes in society, government, politics, and technology, they remain the core values we will abide by.

In an ever-changing world, our core values are constant. Core values are not descriptions of the work we do or the strategies we employ to accomplish our mission. The values underlie our work, how we interact with each other, and which strategies we employ to fulfill our mission. The core values are the basic elements of how we go about our work. They are the practices we use, or should be using, every day in everything we do.

> The lack of core values is a primary reason that very few companies are successful in navigating the challenges of rapid growth.

The lack of core values is a primary reason that very few companies are successful in navigating the challenges of rapid growth.

Early in a company's life cycle, the owner is able to make frequent and personal contact with virtually everyone working inside the company. As the company reaches a certain point in the growth cycle, this personal interaction becomes less frequent, simply due to the workload and other challenges that arise when rapid growth occurs. As human resources, upper-level managers, and midlevel managers are put into place to handle hiring decisions, the owner is further removed from the personnel decision-making process.

In order to ensure that the company continues on a path consistent with the owner's beliefs, it is important to have a set of ethical guidelines. These ethical guidelines tie in with the core values of the organization and are vitally important to the long-term success of the organization.

Organizations are successful because of people who share a common purpose, a common mission, a common vision, and work within a set of common core values. Below are the core values at Pro Food Systems (PFSbrands):

Have fun

Always treat others as you want to be treated

Practice "ownership thinking"

Positive ATTITUDE always

I —There's no "I" in "TEAM"

No complaining

Entitlements do not exist

Structure and balance—God, family, work, and everything else

Straight talk and simple is better

Remember that the customer is why we are here

U never get a second chance to make a first impression

Learn to communicate openly through all channels

Everyone has the opportunity to excel

If you follow the first letters down, you will notice that our core values spell out *HAPPINESS RULE*. As we all live and work by these core values, I guarantee you that our work will be more fun and more rewarding. Furthermore, I will go out on a limb and bet that your personal life will improve as a result of adopting these core values. Let's cover each of these core values in more detail in a way consistent with how they are explained to each employee-owner at PFSbrands. This will help you to better understand why they are important to me and the success of PFSbrands.

1. HAVE FUN

Whoever said work was not supposed to be fun? It's common knowledge that people generally spend more hours working than doing anything else. Some of you may spend more time sleeping than you do at work, but you get my point. Since we all spend so much time working, why not find something that you truly enjoy doing and make it a priority to ensure that you have fun and those who work around you also have fun? For me, the best sign of this is seeing people laughing, joking around, and developing true friendships with people they work with.

As a leader, I've worked diligently to provide an environment conducive to having fun. I admit that sometimes it may not always appear that I am having fun at work. Part of this is because of my somewhat introverted personality, and part of this can be attributed to my work ethic and the high expectations I have of myself. I always tell people that I'm a little "warped" because I truly enjoy working, and I thrive on the constant challenges it presents. I let all of our employees know that it is up to them to make having fun a reality within their job and their department. Why not make it your mission to spread happiness to fellow employees, customers, and vendors?

2. ALWAYS TREAT OTHERS AS YOU WANT TO BE TREATED

The GOLDEN RULE, folks! Most people learned, or were at least aware of, the Golden Rule as a child. There's not much that can be expanded upon here. The rule is simple and clearly stated. Always treat others with respect and reflect back on this core value anytime you feel the need to jump all over someone.

If you are human, at some point you will break this Golden

Rule. When that happens, be sure to make amends by apologizing to the person you treated unfairly. Remember, these rules are especially important when working with your teammates (coworkers). Always approach your teammates in a respectable manner, regardless of the circumstances.

3. PRACTICE OWNERSHIP THINKING

I could write another book on this entire subject, and probably will someday. To try to summarize this briefly, ownership thinking is focusing on the bottom-line profitability of the company and taking care of your employees. While successful companies know that these are closely related, make no mistake about it, a company cannot be successful in the long term without focusing on both areas.

> Ownership thinking is focusing on the bottom-line profitability of the company and taking care of your employees.

A company MUST be profitable in order for an owner to take care of his or her employees. Businesses exist to generate cash. If everyone within the company thinks like an owner and focuses on ways to be more profitable, and the owner is committed to taking care of his or her employees, then everyone has tremendous opportunities to excel.

4. POSITIVE ATTITUDE ALWAYS

Ponder for a moment the most successful people you know. I guarantee you that all of these people carry a positive attitude, always remain optimistic, and have a never-quit personality.

As Americans, we are all fortunate to be protected by the United

States military. At the top of the list many would say are the US Navy SEALs. This is a unique group of individuals who are both mentally and physically tough, extremely intelligent, and always carry a positive can-do attitude. Do you want negative people protecting your life and freedoms? Not only are these Navy SEALs unique as individuals, but they also understand the importance of operating as a unit and team.

I was fortunate to meet a former Navy SEAL commander last year, Roark Denver. Roark was at a CEO conference I attended in Idaho. During his short presentation Roark shared one of the most valuable leadership lessons he learned during his time serving as a Navy SEAL. During his training he had a commander tell his unit that "calm is contagious." The lesson for leaders is to remain calm in stressful situations. Your calmness is contagious and those around you will be more likely to remain calm as well.

I'm also a fan of the book *Extreme Ownership,* written by former SEALs Jocko Willink and Leif Babin. *Extreme Ownership* demonstrates how to apply principles and mind-set to any team or organization, in any leadership environment. A compelling narrative with powerful instruction and direct application, *Extreme Ownership* challenges leaders everywhere to fulfill their ultimate purpose: lead and win.

Like the Navy SEALs, at PFSbrands we aspire to recruit, hire, and retain "A" players. These A players want to succeed, want to perform well, and in general aspire to do a good job and constantly excel.

This does not mean that these people don't make mistakes. Mistakes are part of being human. The difference between A players and others is that A players learn from their mistakes and take corrective actions to make sure the mistakes don't happen again. A players are forward thinking and positive by nature. A players are not always interested in advancement or management type positions, but they do want to be the best at their job and they take pride in making positive contributions to the company. A players have the ability to remain calm in stressful situations or when things may not necessarily be going their way.

Anyone can be or become an A player. It simply revolves around having a positive attitude along with a desire to learn and constantly improve.

> **Anyone can be or become an A player. It simply revolves around having a positive attitude along with a desire to learn and constantly improve.**

5. "I"—THERE'S NO "I" IN "TEAM"

A team is made up of individuals. There are good teams and bad teams. The most successful teams are those who know their teammates so well that they begin to anticipate moves. For a team to be successful it is not necessary to have the most talented players, although this can be a big benefit, if they are coached correctly. The most important part of successful teams is the fact that they work together toward a common goal and everyone realizes their role by KEEPING SCORE. Successful businesses are no different than successful teams. The ones that are successful always know the score and work to improve it.

6. NO COMPLAINING

This is probably one of my biggest pet peeves, and unfortunately our society has become far too accepting of complaining. If you need proof of this, just spend a few minutes on social media and specifically pay attention to those complaining. Needless complaining is a waste of your time and the time of those whom you are complaining to. Furthermore, just like "calm is contagious," so is complaining. Before you know it, the noncomplainers have been sucked into the complaining mentality.

These complainers don't realize they are doing absolutely no good and simply dragging others into their dark hole of negativity. Many will defend themselves by saying it is good to "vent." I couldn't disagree more. I feel it is good to talk about your problems with those who care, but at the same time you should be offering solutions and working toward those solutions that will improve life for everyone. The next time you feel like complaining, think about how you can be constructive in taking the high road to a solution.

If anyone wants to read a quick, short book on this topic, try picking up *The No Complaining Rule,* by Jon Gordan. I guarantee you that it will make you think differently about complaining both at work and in your personal life.

7. ENTITLEMENTS DO NOT EXIST

This goes along with the ownership thinking mentality mentioned above. Remember that in order to take care of employees, an owner must be profitable. In order to ensure long-term sustainability and profits, a company cannot create a culture of entitlement. None of us are entitled to anything ... including me.

Salaries and benefits are based on market conditions, what companies can afford to pay, and what individuals are willing to do the job for. This is "straight talk" (another core value that will be discussed shortly) for saying salaries are based on supply and demand. Neither companies nor managers establish salaries ... the marketplace does.

Raises are not guaranteed every year, salaries are not reflective of time served with the company, and nothing is guaranteed. Those companies that have created, or been forced to create, systems of entitlement will eventually fail, or they may likely move overseas. Entitlement companies may survive through a few generations if they are growing companies. However, there is NO WAY a company can survive long term with a system of entitlement. They are doomed to failure.

I know I am going to offend a few people here, but put yourself in an ownership position and accept the straight talk so you can at least appreciate my opinion. Sick days and bereavement are entitlement programs. Let's address the sick days first, since it's something I'm adamant about *not* implementing at PFSbrands.

> Entitlement companies may survive through a few generations if they are growing companies. However, there is NO WAY a company can survive long term with a system of entitlement.

I realize people are going to get sick and I would prefer that you don't come to work when you are sick. However, why should you be paid when you don't work? Why should someone who is sick for five days get paid for those five days when their teammate didn't miss a day, had to work those five days, and got paid the same wage? Not only that, but while you were out sick, your teammate had to pick up the slack and work twice as hard. Is that fair? NO.

At PFSbrands, we offer extra paid time off (PTO) to compensate for not offering sick days. This allows healthy individuals the opportunity to use these days for vacation or any other personal reasons. If you are sick, it allows you to use the days and still be paid. However, your teammates are getting the same amount of days to use at their discretion. Is that fair? ABSOLUTELY.

Is bereavement an entitlement? Sure it is. It is something that was established as a company benefit that now has come to be expected, and employers get to pay employees for extra time off without productivity. Bear with me through this because I do have a sensitive and caring side. In fact, I care deeply about people. However, is it fair that those with stepfathers and stepmothers, larger families, stepchildren, etc. get more paid time off than do their teammates?

It's not your teammate's fault that you have a larger family, and it certainly is not your employer's fault. Once again, guess who picks up the slack when you need to be gone? That's right, your teammates.

I say all of this only to make a very strong point on entitlements and the overwhelming expectation that is engrained in our culture that make people believe they deserve things. However, my belief in the importance of family outweighs my feeling on not offering this benefit (not entitlement) to all PFSbrands employees. PFSbrands does have a bereavement policy and I am glad to be able to offer it. Death is a difficult time, especially when it relates to immediate family.

Is jury duty an entitlement? I bet you know my answer.

YES, it is a mandated entitlement that requires employers to allow employees off work. I have no problem with allowing employees time from work to serve this great country. However, as an employer, it is not my responsibility to pay employees for the time off work to serve their country. As a United States citizen, it is your duty to serve your country and pay for it accordingly. It's a small price to pay to live in this great country.

I believe in keeping salaries at a competitive level, making sure we do not create long-term overhead burdens for the company, ensuring company stability, and rewarding everyone for company profitability.

There's that "profitability" word again. Why does that keep popping up? Did I mention that none of this stuff matters if we are not profitable? Most people have a misperception about owners and the amount of money they "make" or "take home." The average American believes that businesses take home 36 percent of every dollar of revenue they take in (which is about five times the actual profit).[1] I mentioned that I could write a whole book on the "ownership thinking" value. Entitlement cultures exist in large part because many people simply do not understand the basics of business, taxes, the income statement, the balance sheet, and the cash flow statement.

Part of our work in developing all of these core values involves some financial educational sessions that make everyone more aware of the challenges involved with achieving profitability. Furthermore, this education provides everyone an opportunity to see how they can impact the company's profitability and enhance their opportunity for additional income.

IMPORTANT NOTE ON SALARIES: Remember those A players with positive attitudes mentioned above? They generally earn higher salaries because they are easy to manage, they have a positive attitude, and bosses generally enjoy being around them. Want to earn more money? Work to become an A player.

8. STRUCTURE AND BALANCE— GOD, FAMILY, WORK, AND EVERYTHING ELSE

I bet there are not a lot of employers out there who truly believe work is third on the priority list. However, reality can never be hidden forever.

I realize everyone has a life outside of our company. I also realize that people who manage their personal lives successfully are more

---

1   Mark J. Perry, "The General Public Thinks the Average Company Makes a 36% Profit Margin, Which Is About 5X Too High, Part II," AEIdeas, accessed April 5, 2019, www.aei.org/publication/the-public-thinks-the-average-company-makes-a-36-profit-margin-which-is-about-5x-too-high-part-ii/.

productive when they are at work. This is why I encourage everyone to focus on their personal lives and make time with their families. This is an area that is extremely difficult for me because of the passion and enjoyment I get out of work.

Before Julie and my three daughters chime in and tell me to "practice what I preach," I just want everyone to know that this is an area I have tried to remain conscious of over the years. Like most entrepreneurs, it's also an area where I have struggled to find balance. To help in creating better balance for my family, I have sacrificed a lot of personal activities. I don't hunt or fish, so that's never drawn me away from family time. I've elected not to play golf much, instead opting to use that time to spend with family. In reality, most of my time outside of work is spent creating memories with my family. Because of my work ethic and the success that has come along as a result of it, I've been able to offer some unique experiences for my family. These experiences and memories are far more rewarding than material things.

Entrepreneurs get pulled in a lot of different directions and deal with a lot of stress. As a dedicated leader, I put a lot of pressure on myself to ensure that I make the right business decisions for my immediate family and for my corporate family. I've managed to make time for family vacations and individual vacations with Julie. I've made it a point to coach each of my daughters in at least one sport, I rarely miss a family event, and I've made it a point to always be around for family events each holiday.

There's a stark reality that comes along with being an entrepreneur: you have to be there. You have to be present and you have to work more than anybody else, especially in a start-up business. That creates a dark side to entrepreneurs; many of them become accustomed to and even obsessed with their work. If you are a visionary, the obsessions become greater and greater because you can see the future clearly when others can't. You know where you want to go and you want to get there faster than anyone else. Oftentimes, these things will be hard to control and it takes a massive amount of effort to create balance.

Use your Outlook Calendar and smartphones to your advantage. Schedule all of your personal events on your calendar of choice. If you don't want other individuals to see your personal events, you can always make them "private." If you are career minded and plan to be successful, then I guarantee you that you won't make every one of the personal events you enter on your calendar.

However, if they are not on your calendar, I will assure you that you will be absent at a large percentage of these personal events. Microsoft Outlook, Google, smartphones, and numerous technology applications have helped me to organize my life. Thanks, Bill Gates and Steve Jobs.

Finding structure and balance is extremely difficult even if you don't own a business. Successful people work harder and smarter than do unsuccessful people. Even though my career oftentimes pulled me away from family, it has also allowed me the opportunity to create some unbelievable opportunities and memories for our family. Don't sacrifice a career for the things in life that are more important. Find the right spouse who supports your desire to be successful and find your balance.

9. STRAIGHT TALK AND SIMPLE IS BETTER

By now you've probably seen a theme with our core values. We want to ensure that we all treat each other fairly and with respect,

> Even though my career often times pulled me away from family, it has also allowed me the opportunity to create some unbelievable opportunities and memories for our family.

remain positive and optimistic, don't complain, and have fun. But there comes a time when "straight talk" is a necessity. By this I mean EVERYONE has the right to tell anyone whatever is on their mind, as long as they do it in a constructive and nondestructive manner.

This straight talk approach even means confronting me if there is something that you do not agree with. I will NEVER, EVER fire somebody for a straight talk approach. The only thing I ask for in return is the realization I get to make final decisions, and sometimes these are not easy or popular decisions. I ask all my leaders within the company to lead in the same manner.

Great teams are made up of individuals who are committed to living by and abiding by decisions made by leaders. If a decision is so severe that a person cannot abide by it, then he or she should resign and find a new place to work. I want PFSbrands to be one of the best places to work in the world. However, I realize that it is impossible for me to make EVERYONE happy 100 percent of the time, and I cannot make decisions that EVERYONE agrees with. Any great leader will face this same challenge. Great leaders are not always the most popular or most liked. Great leaders have thick skin. The best advice I can give any leader is to work toward becoming a *servant* leader who is respected. But understand that respect will oftentimes mean decisions are unpopular.

The second part of this core value is "simple is better." We all need to stay focused on keeping everything as simple as possible. Take the game of soccer, for example. Soccer is a simple game—keep your shape, control the ball, and work as a team. Business is a simple game—keep it simple (KIS). Or as some people like to say, keep it simple, stupid (KISS). Or as I like to say, keep it stupidly simple (KISS).

10. REMEMBER THAT THE CUSTOMER IS WHY WE ARE HERE

How many times have you heard someone complain about something a customer is requesting? First, refer to the "no complaining" core value. Second, consider what would happen if we didn't have our customers. I know, it sounds simple and ridiculous, but without our customers there is no need for us to be here. That being said, it's absolutely amazing how many companies don't emphasize the importance of this with their employees, or invest in educating their employees on how to treat customers.

The next time you feel like you *have to* do something, shift your thought process to the fact that you *get to* do something. You *get to* go to work while there are so many people unemployed. You *get to* live in this free country while so many are suffering in other less-friendly environments.

> The next time you feel like you *have to* do something, shift your thought process to the fact that you *get to* do something.

You *get to* wake up today, while so many others have had their lives cut short by illness or tragedy.

Focus on feeling *blessed* instead of *stressed*. Be grateful for the opportunity to live and work. This is really a simple mind-set change that can transform your life. Give it a shot. Make a commitment to changing your mind-set. It will change your entire personality and you will be a much happier person.

IMPORTANT NOTE: Your teammates (coworkers) are also your customers. It's unbelievable how many companies develop silos within their organization. These silos cripple the ability to work as a team. However, when you educate your employees on the fact that their internal customers are just as important as their external customers, amazing results can occur.

11. U NEVER GET A SECOND CHANCE TO MAKE A FIRST IMPRESSION

I have to give another shout-out to my dad on this one. I wish I had a dollar for every time I have heard this saying in my life. Dad was a true motivator, teacher, and mentor for me as it relates to core values. He has spent his entire life helping others, instilling core values, and working for change in the world. I'm blessed to have a father who is a far better man than I am. Luckily for me, he always had (and has) extremely high expectations of me.

Think about the power of this simple saying: "You never get a second chance to make a first impression." This not only holds true when you meet someone for the first time, it also holds true the first time you talk to someone or see someone during the day.

If you make a bad first impression, that sets the tone for the rest of the relationship or the rest of the day, week, month, etc. Always think about the impact you have on someone the first time you meet them or the first time you see them. If you concentrate on this, it will help everyone achieve the first core value: Have fun!

12. LEARN TO COMMUNICATE OPENLY THROUGH ALL CHANNELS

We do a lot of surveys at PFSbrands. Over the years when I have asked what people would change within the company to make improvements, a typical response is communication. This answer is always frustrating to me because I can always agree and disagree with the need to communicate better.

I know, these contradict each other. I think this is a canned response from most people that is generally hiding a bigger issue, and the individual won't provide the "straight talk" to actually get to the root of the problem. However, COMMUNICATION is critical in all companies, especially those that are rapidly growing.

Let's make one thing very clear. I want to be sure there is absolutely no way that this can ever be misinterpreted. ANYONE, AT ANY TIME, CAN CONTACT ME (OR HUMAN RESOURCES) TO DISCUSS ANYTHING. It's that simple. We are not a command-and-control company that only allows people to talk to their supervisor about issues.

It does not matter how big we get, I will always have this open-door policy. I simply ask that my employees attempt to go through their immediate leader (unless a particular issue involves their leader specifically and presents an uncomfortable situation) to address issues.

If the issue is important and does not get resolved, no one should ever hesitate to take it to a higher level. Furthermore, a leader (or anybody for that matter) should NEVER reprimand an employee in any way, shape, or form for being persistent about a problem.

Our company encourages open communication from top to bottom. At no time should anyone feel threatened about copying someone on an email, taking a situation to a higher level of leader-

> I know that if we hire the right people, promote the right people, and live by our core values, uncomfortable issues are going to be few and far between.

ship, or offering "straight talk" to anyone else in the company.

I know that if we hire the right people, promote the right people, and live by our core values, uncomfortable issues are going to be few and far between.

13. EVERYONE HAS THE OPPORTUNITY TO EXCEL

For those of you who don't believe this last core value, I have one suggestion: I highly encourage you to work on the first twelve core values. As a company, if we live and operate under all of these core values, then there is absolutely nothing holding us back. The opportunity to excel comes naturally with growth and will continue to come naturally with focus on these core values.

At PFSbrands, everybody has an opportunity to advance financially and professionally. Occasionally it is important to seek talent from the outside to assist our company with the unique challenges we face as a rapidly growing company. However, I commit to promoting from within as much as possible. Those who have the right attitude, want to succeed, understand and embrace the mission and vision statements, and adopt the core values will have numerous opportunities.

STEP UP TO THE PLATE
Turning Ideas into Action

Unlike at a lot of companies, instilling core values was not a major shift in our company. These core values already resonated throughout our company and within many individuals. Change is never easy and is often resisted. Your culture will not change or improve overnight. It will take a concerted effort on behalf of everyone to make sure you all operate under established core values.

In everything you do, always consider if it coincides with a purpose, mission, vision, and a sound set of core values. If you encounter someone doing something outside of your core values, then it is your responsibility to offer some constructive criticism and/or some straight talk to correct the situation. Focus on the bottom line, have fun, and embrace your core values, and good opportunities will be endless.

At the time I wrote the PFSbrands core values in 2011, I had read that there were roughly 23 million firms in the United States. Only about 4 percent (920,000) of these companies were above $1 million in annual revenue. Only about 0.4 percent (92,000) of *all* companies had made it beyond $10 million in revenue. Only 17,000 companies surpassed $50 million, and a mere 2,500 companies surpassed $500 million in annual revenue. In fewer than twenty years, PFSbrands is already in an elite group of companies and we owe it to a dedicated team and a unique culture that revolves around thinking and acting like an owner.[2]

Where do you think your company will end up on this list?

---

2   Verne Harnish, *Scaling Up: How a Few Companies Make It...and Why the Rest Don't* (Ashburn, VA: Gazelle, Inc., 2014).

Questions to consider:

1. Establish your personal WHY. If you are a company leader, work with your team to establish your company WHY, along with a mission statement, vision statement, and a set of core values. Constantly communicate these to your team.

2. Recall the first person, boss, vendor, or customer who took a chance on you. I'm sure you have thanked them more than once. How are you taking a chance on others?

3. Developing a supply chain, recipes, and packaging are some of the most important key assets in any business, yet, you will not find them on your balance sheet. What are the most important assets in your business not found on your balance sheet? How are you continually investing in and protecting those assets?

4. Developing core values can easily become a check-the-box company activity. Do not let this happen. Accordingly, what are your company's core values? Are they living, breathing, and active? Is the end result staff alignment toward the company's goals and objectives? Why or why not?

5. As an individual, what are your nonnegotiables? What individual core values do you live by daily?

6. If you are a leader, do you have someone working for you that is not a good fit for the company or the job they are tasked with? If so, what are you doing about it?

7. Do you come to work every day with a positive attitude? If not, what are you doing to correct that?

8. Do you consider yourself an A player? If not, what are you doing to get there?

CHAPTER 4

Shaking Things Up: How Being an Industry Disruptor Creates New Opportunities

Status quo, you know, is Latin for "the mess we're in."
RONALD REAGAN

Not too long ago we brought in one of our customers for what we now call Discovery Days. Discovery Days is a two-day event we host at PFSbrands that allows our customers and prospects to get an in-depth look at our entire company. They get to meet our entire team and learn about the massive amount of resources we have created to help our customers become more successful.

When we brought the leaders of this organization into Missouri, they only had three Champs Chicken locations with us. The customer owned a convenience store chain based out of Idaho and had a lot more stores where they were considering installing food-service operations. The president and a few members of his staff politely attended, but they were essentially very close to cutting ties and moving on … that is, until they saw our company in action, experienced our culture, and finally understood all the resources available to them that they weren't utilizing. During the next two years, they added more than a dozen Champs Chicken operations in their stores.

> Doing things differently in any industry is never easy, not necessarily because implementing a new process is difficult, but because changing the mind-set of the masses requires a tremendous amount of time, energy, and resources.

Doing things differently in any industry is never easy, not necessarily because implementing a new process is difficult, but because changing the mind-set of the masses requires a tremendous amount of time, energy, and resources.

I was fortunate to be able to gain a tremendous amount of knowledge during my days at Mid-America Farms about how national food-service brands handled their business and their distribution. As I mentioned, I had the unique opportunity to pioneer Mid-Am's first sales internship and training program while in college. Throughout that process, I got to work in all of their internal departments: Accounting, Customer Service, Procurement, Logistics, and more. I also got to see the operational side of the business, which allowed me to spend time in various factories, to really get an intimate view inside the world of a Fortune 500 company.

This unique opportunity at Mid-Am certainly gave me a lot of business experience. Working in the packaged and process cheese division, I got a look into how some of the best companies in the world handle their food-service needs. I got an inside look at wholesale distributors such as Sysco, US Foods, McLane, Associated Wholesale Grocers, and many more. I worked with food-service buying groups such as Frosty Acres, Golbon, and UniPro. I dealt with processors such as Hormel, Conagra, and Tyson. I experienced working with major retailers like Walmart and wholesale clubs like Sam's and BJ's, and with national chains as well, such as Taco John's, Taco Bell, Chili's, Applebee's, Cracker Barrel, Pizza Hut, Domino's, Little Caesar's, Blimpie, and many more.

Looking back at my time at Mid-Am, I would not change a thing. I got an opportunity to learn from an amazing company and to work under some fantastic mentors. As I think back on many of the conferences and professional events that I had the pleasure of attending on behalf of Mid-Am, I remember several conversations popping up about my age. Most people thought that I was in my early thirties when in reality I was in my early twenties. That was maybe a testament to the way I carried myself and the fact that I was superknowledgeable about the business. I've always had a knack for being able to relate to all kinds of different people, especially when it pertains to business. However, having people guess your age as older was a compliment back then ... not so much today.

In dealing with so many national franchise brands, I gained a true understanding of the distribution side of the business ... and how *controlled* it was.

THE TRADITIONAL WAY

Let's run through the traditional way that successful food-service brands like those listed above get a product to their establishment. While there's a lot that goes into procuring products and getting them distributed, I'm going to give you a very high-level view of how this happens.

Most national food-service chains negotiate directly with manufacturers as it relates to their product formulations and pricing. After the chain has their product pricing negotiated with the manufacturer, they will work with distributors to negotiate a separate agreement that allows the distributor to make a certain percentage for getting the product from the manufacturer to each individual restaurant.

Let's use a stand-alone restaurant franchise as an example. When I say stand-alone restaurant, I mean a restaurant that is either in its own building or has its own rented space inside a larger retail center. Since everyone reading this book will recognize KFC, let's use them as our example. Since KFC is famous for their chicken breading, we will use that product to illustrate the food and distribution chain. We can't possibly cover every step in the process, but this is meant to give a very high-level overview of the steps involved for food products to reach consumers.

First, all those raw ingredients have to get from the farm to a blending facility. The flour comes in a large tanker truck and is pumped into silos that are attached to the manufacturing facility. The flour is then pumped into a large stainless-steel ribbon blender, where all the other spices are generally added by manual labor. After the exact amount of time has elapsed, the mixed breading is either pumped or gravity-fed into bags or boxes. Depending on the automation of the manufacturing facility, the bags or boxes are either manually sealed or automatically sealed, then generally placed on a conveyor and passed through a metal detector.

Many years ago, some of these recipe processes (the actual blending of ingredients) may have been done at each individual store. However, as labor availability has changed over time, most national chains prefer to have their products further prepared by manufacturers. Additionally, as restaurant chains grow in size, it becomes more difficult to control product consistency at the store level if you have complicated processes and recipes for menu items. And, vitally, product consistency can be the difference between success and failure in the restaurant business, and many other businesses, for that matter.

So once the ingredients are properly packed into a bag or a box at the manufacturing facility, they are stacked on a pallet and then shipped off to a distribution company that is ultimately responsible for delivering the breading to the restaurant. The distribution company is now responsible for getting the breading to each KFC restaurant. KFC has already negotiated their distribution rate, so it is up to the distributor to run their operation efficiently in order to be profitable.

The food-service business is extremely competitive. Margins are thin, and volume is critical in all aspects of food service—farming, manufacturing, distribution, and retail. One of the most important things that a franchisor should do for their franchisees is to ensure pricing consistency for their franchisees. By negotiating the pricing separately with the manufacturer and the distribution company, they are generally able to secure lower pricing in both areas due to the volume of business they provide each of them. This also provides consistent pricing to the franchisees, which allows them to better control their retail margins.

I was fortunate to work at Mid-America Dairymen, where I got to truly understand the restaurant distribution system. My role as a regional sales manager allowed me to specifically work with each one of these segments. I got to meet dairy farmers and see the milk coming from the farm, pumped into tankers, and taken to various factories. The milk was then produced into fluid milk, ice cream, yogurt, butter, cheese, or other dairy products. I was personally responsible for selling packaged and processed cheese to manufacturers and distributors, as I mentioned. However, most of my customers were regional or national restaurant chains. I would negotiate cheese contracts with them directly and then they would inform their food-service distributor that they had to purchase these products from Mid-Am. This was something in the industry that we called "forced distribution," meaning the distributor didn't have a choice who they purchased these cheese products from or the price they paid for these products. The distributor had contractual obligations with the national restaurant chain to inventory the necessary products and deliver them to each individual location at the agreed-upon distribution percentage. Again, consistency is absolutely critical in national food-service brands, so securing the manufacturer and distributor agreements is necessary.

THE NONTRADITIONAL WAY

In 2006, as Champs Chicken was beginning to work with wholesalers, I knew that the integrity of the brand was of utmost importance and ensuring that our Champs Chicken operators were profitable was an absolute must. Up until that time, we were delivering products on our own trucks, directly to our Champs Chicken retail operators. We owned the trucks, hired the drivers, and delivered directly to the supermarkets and convenience stores that were licensed to use the Champs Chicken name. This is known in our industry as "direct store delivery," or "DSD." The drivers were direct employees of PFSbrands, and they would roll our products on a dolly into our customers' retail stores.

We did not operate in a stand-alone environment like the one I described earlier in the chapter with the KFC example. We had developed all of our operations inside supermarkets and convenience stores by signing license agreements with independent supermarket and convenience store owners. Our locations today are still mostly inside other stores like this. We call this a business-within-a-business since these operators are already operating a successful retail business in most cases while we help them install another successful business model within. Think of a Starbucks inside a Target for another example of this. Many major national restaurant chains refer to this as their "nontraditional" locations. For PFSbrands, this is our "traditional segment," and we take pride in truly understanding our customers' businesses and fully realize that we only play a part in their overall success.

You may be sensing that we've got some complications here. In fact, you may even be a little confused. We're taking a traditional food-service concept into nontraditional markets, with a traditional procurement and distribution approach. Hopefully, I don't lose any readers here, but this chapter is really geared to help our wholesale partners and our retailer partners to truly understand how unique our business model is. Not only is our approach completely unique, it wasn't easy to put together, nor was it received well by most distributors initially. This was due to the fact that we had, and still have, a unique wholesaler agreement that provides pricing consistency and other specific requirements. Let me further explain by sharing a little more about the distribution and food-service business as it pertains to supermarkets and convenience stores.

Most of you are probably accustomed to seeing branded food-service offerings inside supermarkets and convenience stores. However, it wasn't that long ago that this wasn't the case. In fact, some of you reading this are old enough to remember when convenience stores didn't exist; they were "service stations" where you got your windshield washed, tires changed, and other general car services performed. Supermarkets were places that you would get dry goods, meat, or poultry items to take home to cook. Prepared food inside supermarkets and convenience stores has evolved greatly and we are proud to be constantly innovating in this space.

As food service expanded in these market segments, the specialized distributors that service these supermarkets and convenience stores had to evolve to survive. Change is hard. Those that didn't change went bankrupt or have since been acquired. Supermarket wholesalers have consistently had to bring in more items to support peripheral departments, such as their deli areas, because the items in "the center of the store" are shrinking in volume. Convenience store wholesalers who were traditionally tobacco and candy distributors now have to bring in food-service items in order to meet the needs of their customer base. This means adding refrigerated equipment in their warehouses and within their transportation fleets.

For many of these wholesale distributors, food service is still fairly new, and delivering to a franchise-branded account is completely new. While traditional food-service distributors such as Sysco, US Foods, MBM, and others are accustomed to executing specialized distribution contracts for national restaurant brands, these specialized supermarket and convenience store distributors we deal with are not (or were not) familiar with this needed distribution structure.

In addition, our competitors in this "nontraditional" food-service space are doing things much differently than we are. Many of our competitors offering food-service brands have offered "exclusive marketing areas" to individual business owners. These individual business owners then have to choose their food-service distributors. Both the individual business owners and the food-service distributors have the ability to put whatever markup they want on those products. This not only increases the retailers' food costs, but it almost always presents various prices to each retailer that operates that particular brand. This means there is inconsistency in the food costs that each retailer pays for their goods, thus leading to complications in managing a profitable food-service location. To muddle things further, these "exclusive marketing areas" present even more unique challenges as the independent business owners try to "cross borders" to service their valuable retail partners.

So you can see that there is a flawed model when too many entities in the food-service chain are making money. First, the manufacturer that sold its products to the independent business owner with "exclusive marketing areas" put a markup on the products. Then the independent business owner with "exclusive marketing areas" put a markup on the products to the food-service wholesaler, who's now taking it to the supermarket and convenience store ... with yet *another* markup on the products. That's three different companies that may have complete discretion on what their markup may be. As you can imagine, all three companies have different agendas, priorities, needs, and cash flow requirements—none of which are to ensure that the retailer can be profitable with the branded program.

With multiple markups through this flawed distribution model, the retail operator is now faced with a decision to (a) take a lower gross profit margin than they need to be successful in the food-service business, or (b) set their menu pricing at a level so high that it may force the consumer to decide it just isn't a good value.

I knew that for PFSbrands to survive and build a lasting and sustainable brand, it would be extremely important to control the food costs to our retailers. As noted in our mission statement in an earlier chapter, it is extremely important that our retailers are able to be profitable. I knew that if we didn't have a business model that would help them drive profitability, we really didn't have anything at all. To take it a step further, I also knew that it was critical for our retail partners to be successful for our wholesale partners to continue to exist.

> I knew that for PFSbrands to survive and build a lasting and sustainable brand, it would be extremely important to control the food costs to our retailers.

The last line of our mission statement reads: "Assisting our retail customers in operating profitable locations." And because I had learned how things were traditionally done on a national level, I knew PFSbrands was severely disrupting the industry when we went out with a national pricing strategy, a controlled wholesaler margin, and a unique distribution agreement with our wholesale partners. While the agreement is unique to them, it's actually very common with those broad-line food-service distributors that deal with national food-service brands on a daily basis.

During my early meetings with potential wholesaler partners, the initial response was generally something like, "What? You're telling me that I can only make a certain margin on the items we distribute for you?" As with most businesses, there always seem to be egos involved as well, and many of the wholesalers I met with didn't take kindly to being told what they could sell the product for. They *perceived* the margin was small, despite the fact that it was actually far better than most food-service distributors made with their national chain business. Those wholesalers who truly understood the value that we brought to the table decided to move forward with us. They understood that we were responsible for most of the work from start to finish with every single retail account. The resources we provide our wholesaler partners and our retail partners drive significant volume through our distribution system. Those wholesalers that truly "get it" continue to be our best distribution partners to this day. We respect our partnership with these wholesalers and we're proud to be helping them become more successful in the food-service distribution business, as we feel this is critical to their survival as a wholesale company. I'm also proud to say that I have great personal relationships and friendships with many of these people today. I respect and admire them, while also being grateful to them for taking a chance on me.

Our agreements with our wholesale partners definitely shook things up a bit, but in the end everybody became more profitable. But as far as being a disruptor in the industry, we were just getting started.

BREAKING THE EXCLUSIVE TERRITORY MODEL

One of the most frequently asked questions we get from prospective wholesale distributors is, "Can I have an exclusive territory?"

Here's one of the best responses for a distribution company that is wanting an exclusive territory: Let's say I give you an exclusive territory. What happens if you've got a chain for a customer, and that chain now goes across your exclusive territory lines and starts buying or building stores to expand? You obviously want to grow with them, right? They would like to get our food-service products from you, but the customer's new stores are outside of your territory. In fact, someone else has the rights to that exclusive territory and now a competitor of yours may have the exclusive right to supply that store with our branded products.

At the end of the day, we want all of our wholesalers to be able to follow their customers because it's in everybody's best interest. The customers want that, and the wholesalers want that. Believe me, I've seen firsthand the complications that exclusive territory arrangements cause for everyone involved in the supply chain.

As I stated earlier, our company started as an exclusive distributor for BKI, our equipment company. Remember, we had the "hourglass shape" in Missouri? We loved our exclusive agreement, and in fact begged for it. It was great, or so we thought as long as we were content with being a company that didn't intend to grow beyond this exclusive area. At one point, we had grown our BKI exclusive territory to touch eight states. What happened was eye opening. All of a sudden, we couldn't grow the brand any further geographically. We wanted to sell BKI to a new Champs Chicken licensee in Alabama, but we couldn't. Not unless we convinced BKI to break their exclusive territory model. Or we could pay a fee (penalty) to the BKI distributor that had the Alabama territory. Under the distribution agreement at the time, we would be forced to pay the local BKI distributor a fee and they would be required to do the training on the BKI equipment.

Now you might be thinking: *So what's the problem? Why not just let the local BKI distributor do the training on the equipment?* Remember how critical consistency is in the food-service industry? Of course we didn't want anyone else doing the training, because the reputation and consistency of our product were on the line. While I'm sure the local BKI distributor understood the equipment, they had no idea how to train this location on how to prepare our products. Our staff had to be at this particular store to train on the proper operating procedures for Champs Chicken; we didn't need anyone to train them on the equipment, because we needed to train them our way for consistency purposes. So, under an exclusive territory arrangement, we were forced to pay the local BKI distributor a "fee," even though they did nothing. What does that mean? It means we would have to charge more for the equipment, which would ultimately hurt the retailer because their cost of entry would be higher. With enough of those scenarios, we would ultimately become uncompetitive and therefore unattractive to potential franchisees. Scaling would stop.

Jeff Johnson was our sales representative for BKI at the time and had been a longtime advocate for us. He'd been our representative for years and he could understand the vision that we had to grow Champs Chicken into a national brand. He understood

> **With enough of those scenarios, we would ultimately become uncompetitive and therefore unattractive to potential franchisees. Scaling would stop.**

the challenges we were dealing with, and he also understood the fact that we had grown year over year, double digits plus with BKI, and had always done what we said we were going to do. He saw our company scaling, and he knew where we were headed. Most importantly, Jeff knew our core values and the way we represented BKI.

Thankfully, BKI had a president at the time who had come from a food-service company that did not have exclusive territories, but that didn't necessarily make matters easy. After nine to twelve grueling months of tough conversations, and thanks to Jeff's ongoing advocacy, BKI finally relented and gave us full rein across the country, and in fact internationally, to sell their equipment, as long as it was being installed at a Champs Chicken location. We weren't purposely trying to be a disruptor; we simply wanted to do the best thing for our Champs Chicken retailers while continuing to scale our operation with more consistency and efficiency. The results? We went from purchasing around $500K annually from BKI to more than $2 million.

This was around 2009 when most everyone else was seeing their top-line revenue erode due to the effects of one of the worst recessions in US history. I am not privy to BKI's sales volume with each of their customers, but I'm fairly certain we were the only company showing double-digit growth in equipment purchases through this entire recession.

BEING SELECTIVE

Another misunderstanding in the food-service industry is the fact that when it comes to retail customers, quantity is king. Within the first twelve years, we definitely had issues with what I call "customer churn." We were putting on a lot of retail customers that maybe hadn't been in business very long, or we were signing up customers who weren't committed to consistency and quality. We were actually signing on a lot of customers that, quite honestly, were strictly cost-conscious customers.

Having learned our lessons from that, today in every conversation I have with a potential customer, I very openly say: "If you're looking for the lowest cost of goods, we're not it. We're just flat out not that company. If you're looking for high-quality products and the best service out there, if you're looking for a company that puts people first, is on the cutting edge of technology, and is consistently improving, then we're the company for you. If you're looking for a company that is 100 percent focused on helping you become more successful, then we're the company for you." There are really only two types of business models. You can be a low-cost producer and compete on price, or you can be a high-quality, high-service company that wins business based upon how well you do these things.

Of course we want to keep costs down. The lower we keep food costs for our retailers, the more successful they're going be, thus the more units we're going to be able to establish. But so many companies try to stay somewhere in middle. I firmly believe that you have to pick one strategy or the other—low cost or high quality. The company that gets caught in the middle is the one that will go out of business.

> I firmly believe that you have to pick one strategy or the other—low cost or high quality. The company that gets caught in the middle is the one that will go out of business.

Take Walmart, for example, where the main focus is cost. How can anyone argue with a strategy like Walmart's? They've been extremely successful, but they've been extremely focused on being the low-cost provider. Now take a look at Apple, a company not known for its unbeatable deals, but it has just an absolute, loyal following. In fact, they get three times the amount for an iPad or an iPhone than any of their competitors receive for similar products. Both Walmart and Apple have been successful for many reasons, however neither of them got stuck in the middle of their pricing strategy.

For PFSbrands today, our customer selection process is more like an interview process versus a traditional selling process. We essentially interview our retail customers and try to make sure we get them in the correct space, just like hiring an employee. Because when you hire an employee, you want to make sure that you hire somebody who fits your culture, and just as important, you want to put them in the right lane so they can be successful and excel. When we meet with a potential customer, we are vetting out which program they fit in best, or if they fit anywhere at all. We want only those retailers most committed, the ones who see the value in service, quality, and continuous improvement.

One of the questions I get asked often is, "Why should we do business with your company?" The best answer I can give them is, "Because we're not the same company we were six months ago, and we're not going to be the same company six months from today. If you want the best, if you want a solid brand backed by a solid company, if you want a proven model that works, then our brands are going to survive and thrive over time and through recessions."

EVERYBODY WINS

Speaking of our model, the beauty of it is that it's set up to protect everyone involved. First take our national pricing structure. Our approach with pricing makes it easy for all of our business advisers to know what our retailers' food costs are. The real beauty in having a brand with consistent pricing to operators is when an operator comes to us and says the program doesn't work. We can confidently tell those operators that the program definitely works. If we have successful operators paying the same prices for their cost of goods, then any profitability problem usually comes down to the only thing we can't control. Execution.

The operators have to EXECUTE by following the systems and processes that we've worked so hard to continuously improve over time. We give our operators all of the tools they need to be successful in the food-service business. I get frustrated when anyone tells me that "the program doesn't work." Since our business model is set up the way it is, if the operator is unsuccessful it simply comes down to one of two things: either a poor choice of locations (thus not driving the necessary sales volume) or execution at the store level. It's not the "program." Any operator who wants to blame the program can easily pick up the phone and call some of their counterparts who are showing great success with the program. This goes for wholesalers as well as retailers. We've worked hard to create consistency throughout our wholesaler and retailer network. The most successful wholesalers and retailers are those partners who are truly committed and who work toward flawless execution. Further, they're utilizing our resources and listening to our advice based on our years of experience.

> The most successful wholesalers and retailers are those partners who are truly committed and who work toward flawless execution.

Because our brands are generally operating inside another business, like a convenience store or supermarket, the retailers oftentimes want to operate the food-service operation like the rest of their retail store. If you are a retailer, remember that food service is a different breed and you have to run it like a food-service operation to be truly successful with it. Those who are embracing that concept and putting the right systems and the technology in place, and taking advice from us, are eminently more successful. It also explains why some of our customers may make a 30 percent margin, and others are getting more than 50 percent margin, though they're all paying the same cost for goods. The fact is you can lose money very quickly in the food-service business. Portion control, too much waste, theft—those things just kill you. Not to mention failing to manage your labor correctly.

THRIVING IN A POOR ECONOMY

I think back to the time frame at the end of 2011, when we were in a relatively bad situation, trying to figure out what the heck was going on. In one year, we had added more than $8 million in sales but only $100K in additional bottom-line profit. Yet when I consider the state of the economy at the time, having just gone through 2009 and 2010, the second worst recession in the US history, I find a different perspective and I am thankful. In those two years we nearly doubled our business, while other companies were losing half their sales and trying to figure out how to survive.

We were a rare company during the recession that saw year-over-year sales increases. In fact, as of this book writing, we are proud to say we've had nineteen years of double-digit sales growth. I attribute this to the fact that we've stayed focused on BRANDS, rather than diluting our focus in different areas. While we grew, many companies were struggling. In fact, several went out of business. We feel that we've been successful over time because we are disruptors in our industry, we consistently think outside of the box, and we constantly add more personnel and more services rather than getting stuck in the middle with a pricing strategy. We work to make others more successful.

The bottom line, become a disruptor or someone else will. Don't settle for the status quo. Question the collective groupthink of your industry and consider being a contrarian like I was. Take Amazon, for instance. They've become a disruptor by eliminating the middleman as much as possible and controlling margins.

Like every great disruptor, you need to have a secret ingredient. Ours happens to be:

PEPPER

People

- Find committed partners who will fully support fresh food
- Work to hire the right people in the right places
- Commit to learning from those who know what it takes to be successful
- First find the right WHO and then do WHAT—always PEOPLE FIRST

Equipment

- The right equipment in any food-service environment is critical.
- Automatic-lift fryer
- Automatic-sifting breading table
- Hot case
- Rethermalizer
- Kiosk

Products

The right products take years to develop. Products must be high quality and consistent.

Processes

Standard operating procedures (SOPs) for daily, weekly, monthly, and annual tasks must be in place.

Execution

- Pre-opening planning, project management and training are crucial
- Regular store visits are critical to ensure any food-service program is executed properly

Resources

To be a successful partner with a company dedicated to service!

- Business advisors
- Business developers
- Store design/layout
- Project management
- Marketing team
- Print shop
- Customer success team
- Equipment division
- HR team
- Technology team

STEP UP TO THE PLATE
Turning Ideas into Action

Don't get so much tunnel vision that you're just doing business like everybody else, or just doing things the same way. Find a differentiator. Find something that's unique. Don't try to be all things to all people. Don't get stuck in the middle. Figure out your strategy.

Not everybody is going to like your business model, including your salespeople. We have had, and we continue to get, salespeople who get frustrated when they can't sell to everybody, when they didn't get that deal. We're walking away from more deals today than we ever have, just because we know exactly the type of customer we're looking for. But we're doing a better job with putting the right customers on board with us, those that want to improve, want to get better, and want to become more successful.

Questions to consider:

1. A value chain occurs where raw materials or ideas are captured and then delivered in a new state, adding value to the end customer. How has your business created a value chain that is rare, important, and hard to replicate by others?

2. Who are your most important value chain partners and how are you protecting those relationships?

3. Are you a disruptor or following the crowd in your industry? What can you be doing today that's new and innovative? If you are an employee, this thinking applies to you. What new ideas and energy are you bringing to the office each day? Or are you just showing up?

4.   Do you have a simple framework that captures how you deliver success similar to the PEPPER framework? Use PEPPER as a guide to flesh out the three to five tools and activities that drive success in your business or position.

CHAPTER 5

Opening the Books: How Open-Book Management Helps Your Team Keep Score

---

Tell me and I forget. Teach me and I remember. Involve me and I learn.

BENJAMIN FRANKLIN

One of our employee-owners recently emailed me to share the effect that Open-Book Management (OBM) has had on his family:

I know I've told you about how our house is an Open-Book household and how my kids buy into the process. Well, I came home yesterday, and they had updated the infamous white-board and explained to me that they noticed we have had some increased liabilities and thought we should look at cutting down our clothing, restaurant, and entertainment budgets to get things closer to where they were originally planned. I agreed, and we are looking at areas we can trim the bills, shop providers of our services like internet and phones, as well as find additional revenue opportunities. Sound familiar?

My sixteen-year-old started off by telling me we have lots of things we don't use, so they are putting together a list of items to sell to help pay for the unplanned expense of the broken tub faucet that occurred this week. So, that was updated this morning in the "how will we pay for it" column.

I knew you would appreciate the buy-in at such a young age from my kids. My sixteen-year-old is actually the driver of the whiteboard. She really gets ownership thinking. In fact, her boyfriend complained yesterday that after working on a car for hours, he had to go to work for another eight. She responded with, "You have bills to pay and you need to contribute to your family's cash flow, so off to work you go. Welcome to adulthood." It's even funnier as they are both only sixteen. But this attitude is also why they tolerate me working hours at home on weekends and evenings ...

> **Open-Book Management (OBM) is a method of running a company by engaging all employees in the financial picture of the business.**

For the uninitiated, Open-Book Management (OBM) is a method of running a company by engaging all employees in the financial picture of the business, not simply the C-level executives and accounting department. The theory is based on the premise that if everyone at every level and in every department has their collective finger on the pulse of the financial forecast, all will become much more invested and involved in the overall fiscal health and outlook. Productivity will go up, commitment and loyalty will blossom, and the company becomes stronger. In fact, according to an article in *Forbes,* "Companies register as much as a 30% increase in productivity and profitability in the first year alone, when they implement the approach properly … At [OBM] companies, employees learn to think like owners—which means they behave and act like owners at work and when dealing with customers."[3]

The previous email demonstrates on a small scale what can happen when everyone is involved in the financial picture.

THE AHA MOMENT

Prior to adopting OBM, the culture of PFSbrands wasn't broken by any means. It wasn't a distressed or unhealthy culture. The pace at which we were growing was definitely extreme. We were at a point where we were just adding bodies because we knew we needed people to do things, but we really had no formalized training process, no way to onboard people properly.

We were sharing information, but we were certainly not teaching anybody about the financials. We'd basically just show our top-line sales, and I was judging our company based on top-line sales. What's the growth number look like?

The real aha moment for me came from reading Jack Stack's book *The Great Game of Business* and finally realizing that the majority of employees might be stellar at what they do, but they simply don't understand business. They don't know what they don't know. It's like putting a team of players out on the football field, but they don't know the rules of the game. They may know how to kick or pass or block,

---

3   Bill Fotsch and John Case, "The Business Case for Open-Book Management," *Forbes,* July 25, 2017.

but how can you expect your team to go out there on the field and win when they really don't know the rules?

> How can you expect your team to go out there on the field and win when they really don't know the rules?

I read that book over a weekend and was raring to go first thing Monday morning. I wanted to start assigning general ledger codes and teaching everyone in the company about financial literacy. At that time in November 2011, we had one controller who was basically our entire accounting department. I went in and said, "I need you to read this book because I'd like to implement a lot of these practices. One of the first things we need to do is assign every one of our general ledger codes to an employee. Just read the book and you'll understand."

Well, I wasn't exactly specific on a time frame to read the book. About a week later I checked back in. "Have you read that book yet?"

"Oh, no, I haven't started it."

I remember thinking: *I read this thing over a weekend. I was sure you'd have it done already so we can start the process.* But instead, I said, "Okay, can we maybe knock this out in a couple of days?"

To be fair, she was in the same position as everybody else at PFSbrands during that period—major growth, new changes sweeping in, trying to figure out how to keep up and clean everything up. In the end, it took her a little longer to read the book than I would have liked, and the implementation of OBM moved along more slowly than I wanted. That's not unusual for me because I'm not exactly the most patient person on the planet. I did feel that I needed to get some more buy-in on this whole OBM idea, though.

But first, I kept throwing more change toward our controller. "We've got to close the books quicker. I'm not getting my numbers and financial reports until twenty-five to thirty days after the month has ended. Sometimes, it's forty-five days. We just can't operate like that."

In response, I got all the typical excuses of why we can't close the books sooner. "We can't do it any quicker. We have to wait on expense reports. We have to wait for all of the supplier invoices to come in. We're waiting on this, we're waiting on that."

I thought to myself: *If it takes this long at our size, what will it take to close the month out when we get bigger? This is not going to work. We have to get this month-end closing process down to less than a week.*

Long story short, I had a controller who just wasn't fully on board with the concept of OBM and wasn't fully embracing the change that needed to occur. She didn't particularly like change, either. Our controller was a fantastic individual and I still respect her to this day. However, she just wasn't capable of taking this department to the level I knew we needed to get to. Unlike many founders, I am an owner who is in tune with the numbers. I understand them. After all, I did all of the accounting work myself before I hired her, so I understood the entire process. The problem is that a lot of business owners aren't in that unique position where they truly understand the numbers, or even understand the things that have to be done. Sometimes, when you don't know something, it's easy to second-guess how things can and should be done. It's also easy for someone in a leadership position to feed you false information when they don't want to change.

What I've come to know now is that companies that implement OBM find a serious stumbling block if their accounting department (or accounting individual) isn't totally on board with it. Why? Because many people on the accounting team feel threatened and think that they may not be needed if the company moves to OBM. This is completely false.

In fact, our accounting department has consistently grown in size, and today we have a bigger team of talented personnel in this department than we've ever had. To make OBM run like a well-oiled machine in your company, you need to have an accounting department that's willing to teach people, to become educators. Not that we want everybody to be accountants, but at the very least everybody has to be financially literate enough to understand the numbers. So, it's imperative to have an accounting department that has that instructor mentality.

As a quick sidebar, we routinely close our books completely and accurately by the seventh day of the next month, which is when I get our financial statements. Even better, I get a first glance look at an income statement on the first day of each month, everything down to the gross margin is typically 100 percent accurate and the net income is projected extremely close. Could it get any better than that? You bet. What if I told you that our company has gotten so good at forecasting that I have a solid idea of our total company profitability before the current month even ends?

> **What if I told you that our company has gotten so good at forecasting that I have a solid idea of our total company profitability before the current month even ends?**

So really it doesn't matter what size company you are, the books can be closed and they can be closed timely and accurately. Closing the books each month is simply a matter of developing a checklist of things that must get done and having the persistence to knock it out after each month ends. It's all about systems and processes.

UNDERSTANDING OBM

Obviously, I read a book over a weekend, then came in on Monday and started implementing OBM. So why isn't OBM more mainstream and more widely accepted? It's certainly gaining ground, but why is OBM still a long way off from the preferred business model?

In a majority of cases, the answer is simple: ignorance and fear.

Although some C-level executives and CPAs may have heard of OBM, you shouldn't overestimate the number of people who truly don't understand what Open-Book Management is … *and what it isn't.* The following table highlights the key drivers of OBM:

IT IS	IT IS NOT
• Common sense	• Easy
• Commitment to learning and teaching	• Taught once and forgotten
• Always sharing the reality of the company	• Communicating only the good news
• Rewards and recognition	• An entitlement program
• Financial literacy and education	• A team full of accountants
• Developing organizational trust	• A scheme to trick employees
• Creating better enagagement and growth	• Going away

To illustrate the lack of awareness as it pertains to OBM, our CFO of PFSbrands, Trevor Monnig, recently attended a software conference hosted by the makers of the specific software we use to manage our company. The goal was to discuss a strategic partnership in regard to our new coaching company. Essentially, we needed to be able to offer tools to our clients that can help them with their OBM practices, and in turn we'd be bringing in potential customers for this software company.

Trevor conservatively estimates that he spoke to around thirty people from the software company, throwing out his pitch about a strategic partnership. He explained how PFSbrands utilizes their software as a tool for implementing OBM. Over and over, every single person he spoke with gave him that deer in the headlights look. He didn't have one person say, "Oh, I've heard about that, and it sounds really cool." Or, "Hey, can you tell me more about that?" Or, "I've got a friend that's in a company that practices OBM." Zero out of thirty.

One of his other tasks was, "I want to meet somebody that's using this tool and practicing Open-Book Management." He asked every person he ran across with a name tag from the software company. The response?

"What's Open-Book Management?"

> Ignorance can't necessarily be helped. You can't expect people to know what they don't know. Fear, however, is a different story.

Although that reply may sound shocking to some, it wasn't to Trevor. Prior to his initial interview with PFSbrands, with all his experience and his extensive background in accounting and finance, *he'd* never heard of OBM. Trevor was one of those who just didn't know what he didn't know, even with an MBA.

Ignorance can't necessarily be helped. You can't expect people to know what they don't know. Fear, however, is a different story.

A lot of owners are afraid that OBM means that their competitors are going to get their numbers, and that's somehow going to damage their company. Or that their suppliers and customers are going to see the numbers and think their company is making too much money, or maybe not making enough money. Or even worse, that their employees finally get a peek at the profit margin and decide to revolt.

To address these fears, allow me to defer to Patrick Carpenter, the president of GRITT Business Coaching, which is majority owned by PFSbrands. Patrick's thirty-year career includes senior management positions with two global Fortune 100 companies and international business assignments in Canada, Brazil, Mexico, and the UK, where he opened offices and launched new products. Patrick also co-owned his own medical business, which he grew from $1 million in revenue to more than $12 million in revenue in four years. He just happens to be the son of the late Jill Carpenter, who helped to pioneer the concept of Open-Book Management, coauthoring two books, *The Power of Open-Book Management* and *The Field Book of Open-Book Management.* Prior to taking on the role as president to help launch GRITT Business Coaching, Patrick spent ten years with the Great Game of Business, where he worked as a coach and business developer, helping companies across the globe to implement OBM.

For all those thinking of implementing OBM but who are too afraid of what people are going to think of the numbers, Patrick says the following: "The reality is they think you're making a whole lot more than you actually are."

Patrick is spot on. The misperception of the gross profit margin in a company like ours is actually in the 70 percent range, meaning most employees think we are making a 70 percent gross profit margin. I know this because I personally conduct an educational session where I ask this question of employees who are new to our company. Believe it or not, most people actually think that if we sell a case of chicken tenders for $10, we made $7 gross profit on it. Think again. It's actually about $3, which is a 30 percent gross profit margin. That's just *gross profit margin*. Sales minus COGS (cost of goods sold) equals gross profit. As a company, we still have to pay all of our expenses. After these expenses are factored in, the sale of that $10 case of chicken tenders results in less than 30 cents in *net income* (gross profit minus expenses equals *net income*). This means our *net income* percentage (the "bottom line") is roughly 3 percent (30 cents divided by $10). While all companies achieve different gross profit and net profit percentages, the reality is that many businesses deal with margins such as this. At PFSbrands, we've actually never hit a net profit number as high as 5 percent, and this is not uncommon for many types of businesses.

Tax impact is another huge misperception. Take a poll and most people are going to say that your business pays 10 or 15 percent in federal and state income taxes combined. You'll get a few people who will say 25 or 30 percent. Very rarely do you have anybody say over 30 percent. In reality, by the time both their federal and state income taxes are paid, successful businesses write checks that total nearly 50 percent of their net income (note: tax laws are constantly changing and this can vary based upon the type of corporate structure you have). So if you show a net income of $2 million, you have to pay nearly $1 million taxes. That's a big number and most people are absolutely stunned when they learn the real facts about income tax rates.

> By the time both their federal and state income taxes are paid, successful businesses write checks that total nearly 50 percent of their net income.

The bottom line: fear and the lack of financial literacy are actually working against owners.

CONNECTING THE DOTS

Back to our CFO, Trevor Monnig, who leads many departments in the continuous improvement of our business operations. He not only heads up the accounting team, but also leads purchasing, data analysis, and technology. He has spent more than fifteen years in the role of CFO for two high-growth companies in the manufacturing and distribution industries and prides himself on being a progressive CFO who goes above and beyond the traditional finance roles. Trevor recognizes people as the company's biggest asset and leverages this by hiring for culture and nurturing healthy working relationships. He is experienced in deploying Open-Book Management and firmly believes this transparent platform is the future of organizational management.

But one of his most important roles is to educate our teams on financial performance, financial literacy, and factors impacting the business, and connect each employee-owner to the profitability of the company.

Years ago, during his interview process, Mark Gandy and I took Trevor to lunch to get to know him a little better. Because he's a financial guru, I let Mark ask many of the questions. Trevor was doing great, holding his own. And then Mark asked him if he was a reader. Trevor's face went all shades of pale. Just like me, Trevor had gained experience and knowledge through different experiences, bouncing around different employers, seeing different environments. Seeing things that worked, things that didn't work.

"Well, in full disclosure, no, I am not a reader," he said. "Just less than a month ago, my wife and I were at dinner with another couple and we were on this topic. They were all readers. I told them I had read a grand total of three books in my life, one of them being *The Old Man and the Sea*, by Ernest Hemingway."

Mark and I looked at each other and just laughed out loud. That was one of the two books I had read throughout my entire life before I met Mark. But Trevor was willing to learn, and even more importantly, he was willing to teach.

Business books in Shawn's office.

I had grown up in a family of businesspeople. Yet like many of our employee-owners, Trevor did not. He says that's what gave him an insider's perspective of what it would take to reach the uninitiated.

"I got exposed to the higher levels of business through boardrooms and things like that," he says. "Shawn has mentioned how he doesn't go to Thanksgiving or Christmas without talking about business all day. That's the last thing we ever talked about in our household. We don't have any business owners. Those folks, my grandma and grandpa, my aunts and uncles, are not business owners. So they're in that boat of 'they don't know what they don't know.' And if no one ever takes the time to share it, how would anybody ever learn?

"The key," Trevor says, "is to sit down, explain, and connect the dots. These are dots that many people don't even know exist, so you have to get those dots out there for them first, and then connect them, help them walk the path of understanding business better. I'm very passionate about it; it's a lot of fun for me. I love to help people. I love to see them improve in their professional and personal lives. And I'd say helping them gain financial literacy certainly covers both of those realms. And that's what makes my job really special. But you can only bring it to them. They have to consume it, they have to be willing to go through the door.

"Remember those connect the dots games when you were a kid? You can't see what the picture is supposed to be until you draw a line from dot to dot, in a certain sequence, until you finally see that you've drawn a house or a dog or a car. I firmly believe that people want to be in the know. And when they're not in the know, what do they do? They create their own data points of what they know, or *think* they know. They make assumptions, draw conclusions, and start connecting the dots with other dots that aren't supposed to connect.

"Just imagine playing connect the dots while only having access to some dots and being left to guess where others are supposed to be. Imagine one friend tells you to place a few dots here, and another suggests placing a few dots there. Pretty soon, you're trying to work with what you have to create a picture, and you find that you've drawn a flower when the real picture is a Studebaker. So if we share the dots, if we share the goals, if we share the current data points and the future data points, then we've helped everyone to connect the dots, which creates the big picture everybody can see, without assumptions or misperceptions."

Trevor couldn't be more accurate. We just can't have 130 employee-owners creating dots and pictures that are all different. That's one of the problems for companies refusing to implement

OBM. An owner may look back and say, "Wow, how did this go so wrong?" And nine times out of ten it's because they didn't share the vision well enough for their employees to understand the data points.

> In its simplest form, Keeping Score is making a policy of keeping people in the know.

It all comes back to Keeping Score. In its simplest form, Keeping Score is making a policy of keeping people in the know. And that might start with just sharing what's going on in a quarterly or a monthly meeting.

At PFSbrands, we share what's going on in a company-wide meeting each month, and in each department weekly (even in some departments, daily). But it's all about telling people the score, essentially what's going on in the business. What are different departments doing? If we don't do that, how can someone who is working in the warehouse know what marketing is doing? How would marketing know what the business development team is doing to improve the top line? Or how logistics is trying to be more efficient and drive profitability? So if we share the initiatives that people are working on, and if everyone is Keeping Score and making it visible, then people start seeing, and start tracking, and start to take ownership over wanting to help drive those numbers.

As we connect those dots into future dots, we paint a picture of where the company is going and how we're going to get there. And they are Keeping Score along the way. When people are following along, when they're in the know, they know where we're doing well and, in turn, where we're struggling. They know where we failed. They know where we won. It's that simple. When they're not in the know, I guarantee you that they will make something up.

FINANCIAL LITERACY

At PFSbrands, we established a Financial Literacy Committee, a group of eight people, including a chair and a co-chair. The education really exploded within our company because we're doing creative things to teach our teams about the financials, things like games and competitions. At the end of the day, not everybody needs to be an accountant. The fact is, even simple concepts like debits and credits scare people. I personally hated accounting in high school and college when it got into this debit and credit stuff.

Trevor always tries to break down those barriers of accounting and mitigate any fears.

"Debits and credits are nothing to be afraid of," he tells our employee-owners. "It actually just means left and right. Debit means left, credit means right. One of my favorite things to tell people is, 'Guys, what we're doing here is income statements, balance sheets, and cash flow. Cash flow is critical. That's where we have to get you. You have to understand cash flow at some level and how you impact cash flow. In order to get to there, it's only a matter of addition and subtraction. It's not even multiplication and division. Raise your hand if you can add and subtract. Everybody can do that. I'm not going to ask you to multiply. I'm not going to ask you to divide. It's straight up.' The goal is to keep it as simple as you possibly can."

We teach a five-line income statement. We do start to go a little bit deeper into some tools. Some hands-on things. We created some blocks that illustrate the five-line income statement. Income, cost of goods sold (COGS), gross profit, expenses, earnings before taxes (EBT). We literally throw those on a table and say, "All right guys, this is our income statement. It's a five-line income statement. Let's put it in order."

"That's just as simple as you can get," says Trevor. "We walk through that five-line statement. Then we start to layer things on. It's really about repetition. I think that's one of the key things to remember about financial literacy for people who are not accountants and possibly scared of numbers: repetition is critical. So we constantly start over. Repeat, repeat, repeat. This is electricity. Does that bring in revenue? Is it COGS, or is it an expense? We start breaking it down, and they begin putting their hands on pieces and sliding them into the right spot on the table. People start talking, collaborating together. Even the people at the back of the room who stay away early start looking in a little closer. It's a process. Some people engage faster than others. And all of a sudden, they do it a lot faster than they did the time before. Then we throw out other things that are relevant to our business; we break out different types of revenue. Product revenue, equipment revenue, things like that. Expenses, electricity, health insurance, payroll, etc."

Eventually we pull out a stack of invoices to begin to apply their newfound knowledge to the real world. They can see what went out on a truck and how much revenue was on there. They can see the numbers.

"Wow, that truck had $90,000 worth of product?!" someone might say. Trevor specifically pulls some expensive incoming product loads like catfish, a $120,000 truckload. Those numbers start to make an impact. We pull out an electricity bill from the middle of the summer, or our internet bill. Their average monthly bill for internet at home is probably $40. To service a company like PFSbrands, ours is in the thousands of dollars.

We tie it to their world and before long they're Keeping Score. They now know if we're winning, losing, or tied at any time. A football team does not play the same in the fourth quarter if they're down twenty points or they're up twenty. They need to have different strategies based on the score, and so does a successful business.

To circle back to our opening story, the thing that I think hits home with a lot of people is personal finance. We can all relate to it. I've asked this question in large groups and small groups: "How many people here personally have an income statement or a balance sheet?" Very few hands go up.

If we can walk them through how to do their own personal planning and their own income statement and balance sheet, we are on the road to implementing OBM successfully. How much income do you have coming in? What are your expenses? What is your net income at the end of the month? What's your disposable income? We can then start to feed into, and work into, the balance sheet, which would include all the loans and credit card debt.

Our ultimate goal is to get them to understand that an income statement reports our profitability over a given period of time, that the balance sheet tells us what we own and what we owe at any given point in time. We have to educate everyone on the fact that businesses exist to generate cash and we MUST generate that cash flow to create stability, grow share value, and pay out profit distributions. That's not turning them into a CPA; that's getting them where they need to be to effectively start Keeping Score while understanding the rules of the game, so they know *how* we can all win together.

TAKING ACTION

Businesses exist to produce profits. More importantly, businesses exist to generate cash flow after creating customers. Without cash flow, businesses fail. When businesses fail, people lose their jobs and the company obviously has no ability to create new jobs. I'm not sure why more leaders don't communicate and teach the importance of cash flow. As a business leader, you need to understand that most people don't understand this simple concept and most people have an internal perception that companies are making much more profit than they actually are. If you are a business owner or a business leader you have to trust me here. MOST PEOPLE DON'T UNDERSTAND BUSINESS. Even many of the employees that you assume understand business—they don't. Become a teacher and educate your people.

Diversity plays a big role in organizations as employees represent different backgrounds and different beliefs. These employees are from different communities, and, most of all, they have many different ways to communicate. Communication is key in almost every relationship and relationships in the workplace are no different—relationships play an integral part of the culture within an organization.

An open-door policy, sitting down with employees frequently, having accessible management, and treating others with mutual respect are avenues we use at PFSbrands to keep communication open. We believe in straight talk and when combined with our Open-Book Management, most employee-owners feel valued and respected. Too often, busy executives and managers find it difficult to remain efficient and productive when maintaining accessibility to all employees. We believe processes should be in place so that all employees have opportunities to sit down and discuss issues that affect their job, their lives, and the overall workplace. Our employee-owners are encouraged to meet problems head-on and not turn to other outlets to express concerns. We are dedicated to improving our culture even in the midst of an evolving world.

I've found that there are many benefits that come along with Open-Book Management; high-level communication is one of the most profound. I'm proud to be part of a team that embraces straight talk, encourages all types of communication, and is constantly pushing to get better.

If you are a business owner or leader and scared of Open-Book Management, start by creating and showing your employees some key performance indicators (KPIs). Teach them how these KPIs affect the company and show them how their efforts can affect the numbers. Be patient and remember that this is likely new to most employees. While it seems simple to you as a leader, realize that it is not simple to them. Set the expectations for each employee, establish goals, and help them write their goals down. Create a "scoreboard" with these KPIs that is visible to everyone who walks by. You'll be amazed how people respond when they know the score and actually know their expectations while seeing how their contributions make an impact on the numbers.

If you fully believe in the Open-Book Management approach, good for you. The best advice I can give you is to TAKE ACTION. There are some best practices for implementing OBM and people who can help. I decided to self-implement OBM by combining best practices from some of the greatest thought leaders in the world. I made a lot of mistakes along the way and it took me far longer than I anticipated to get our employees engaged. However, I learned a lot from those mistakes and by self-implementing, we developed a one-of-a-kind system.

I meet too many people that read about OBM and think, "That sounds like a commonsense way to run a business," but then they keep running their businesses the same way.

The key is to TAKE ACTION.

STEP UP TO THE PLATE
Turning Ideas into Action

I started this chapter with a quote from Benjamin Franklin: "*Tell me and I forget. Teach me and I remember. Involve me and I learn.*" Find a way to involve your employees more with your business. Share as much information as you are comfortable sharing with those who are closest to you, your direct reports. As owners and business leaders, we oftentimes fear that everyone is "out to get us." Recognize that most people want to be involved and they want to perform their job well. If you just read that last sentence and scoffed, you've probably not got a great culture and are not dedicated to hiring the right people. The reality is that most of the time we're not giving our workers the tools and knowledge they need to be successful.

Questions to consider:

1. What is OBM, in your own words?

2. Is OBM being practiced in your business? Why or why not?

3. If you could implement OBM in your business, how do you think that would impact your business?

4. Who are the catalysts in your company that could make OBM a mainstay in your company? Will your leadership team support OBM?

5. If you are uncomfortable with OBM, what about sharing the most important key performance indicators for your company, sharing them with everyone, and showing each individual how they can affect at least one of them?

6. Are you having trouble attracting and retaining employees? If so, OBM may help because it creates better engagement.

CHAPTER 6

The Rhythm of Goal Setting: How Small Steps Drive Big Results

---

Most people overestimate what they can do in one year and underestimate what they can do in ten years.

BILL GATES

I wrote down my first major life goal at age twenty-two, the week I was to graduate from college. It hadn't been two months since I asked Julie to marry me. I was working at Mid-America Dairymen, but I still had not been given a full-time employment offer. You can imagine all the feelings going through my head—newly engaged and trying to figure out how I was going to support a family. I knew I liked business, but other than that I really had no idea what the hell I wanted to do with my life.

So I scratched "I want to own my own business by the time I'm twenty-eight" on a piece of paper and tucked it away in a nightstand drawer. I have no idea why I picked age twenty-eight, but I would keep this number in my head over the years that followed.

A few circumstances in my life brought about this particular goal. First of all, I thrived on pressure and competition, and there's no greater pressure and competition than owning your own business. There's no doubt that a childhood spent competing in athletics fueled my desire to consistently measure myself against others and to always be conscious of what the score was. I thrived on the pressure associated with winning. I was in my comfort zone and at my best when I was on the baseball field. When the game was tight, and our team needed something good to happen, I wanted to be at the plate when we needed that big hit, or I wanted to be the one that the ball was hit to when we needed that critical out.

After spending some time with Julie's dad, I saw what he had done, the success he had in owning his own business, and that really strengthened my desire to do something on my own. And with the way I was raised, I knew I had the work ethic. Dad and Mom had always done entrepreneurial-type things on the side—rental investments, farm properties, and fixer-upper homes, to name a few. During my high school years, they renovated an old country club to create a fitness center with an indoor pool, with twelve apartments attached to it. They also later owned a residential care facility for several years. At the time, I didn't know how lucky I was that working hard and taking risks were just a way of life in our family.

But I think one of the biggest influencers along the way happened when I was about sixteen. Dad's full-time employment during most of my childhood involved working for the Presbyterian Children's Home in Farmington, Missouri, where he spent his time helping abused and neglected children. After nearly fifteen years there, one day he was suddenly let go. An entire career spent serving children, dedicating his heart and soul to one company, and somebody else decided it was over.

He was passionate about helping children and helping them become more successful in life. He wanted to stay in the same field and was extremely well respected in Missouri, in fact throughout the entire country. He was quickly offered a position to become the director of Good Samaritan Boy's Ranch, which was about three and a half hours away on the other side of the state. Dad held that position for several years and did a lot of great things for the ranch and the boys who lived there, yet even though he was three-plus hours away, he never missed one of my basketball or baseball games.

That really left an impression on me. I realized there is a certain vulnerability in working for someone else. Of course, our economy is structured to depend on those things. Without a workforce nothing would ever get done. But for entrepreneurs at heart, there's a certain draw to want that freedom, that security, that peace of mind, and that opportunity to grow. The thought of not having to report to somebody else or put my fate in another's hands manifested itself into the note I scribbled down and stuffed into that nightstand drawer. I wanted the opportunity to control my own destiny. I also wanted to be the leader who others depended on to "make that big play" and ultimately win the game.

> For entrepreneurs at heart, there's a certain draw to want that freedom, that security, that piece of mind, and that opportunity to grow.

I beat my goal by four months. In July 1998, I incorporated Pro Food Systems (now doing business as PFSbrands). This would be the first of many goals that I would accomplish in the years to come.

SETTING A RHYTHM

There is setting a goal, and then there is executing it. Though I hadn't realized it, one thing I needed to establish early on was the ability to scale to a medium-sized company and ultimately turn it into a larger company through an ongoing business rhythm. According to the website www.whatissixsigma.net, rhythm can be defined as "a set of pre-defined processes of communication and interactions that should be present between different departments to ensure that the flow of operations is not interrupted and is controlled as intended. It provides a structured way of communication through which the stakeholders communicate to the project team/operations and vice versa on items like roles, milestones, outcomes, targets, and so on that is aligned to the organization's vision."

> Until you create a purpose around the meeting and make sure they start on time, end on time, and are brief when they need to be, you're simply wasting time and productivity.

The problem, however, was that I wasn't much of a systems or process guy. Not only was I lacking these skills, but I was just anti-meeting in general. Drawing from my days spent with Hays Food Systems and Mid-America Dairymen, I personally felt that meetings were a waste of time. Why? Because most of the meetings I'd been in *were* a waste of time. Until you create a purpose around the meeting and make sure they start on time, end on time, and are brief when they need to be, you're simply wasting time and productivity.

Needless to say, we really didn't have many meetings early on with PFSbrands. My philosophy at the time was: if you need to discuss something, go one-on-one with somebody and just tackle the issue. In some circumstances, I still believe that this is the best approach. You have to be willing to tackle an issue one-on-one when the situation calls for discretion or a direct response. As a small company, this one-on-one approach can work great. However, as a founder grows their business, the time available to spend with each employee becomes less and less. In time, I learned that as the leader of a company, you need to leave much of that type of communication to the key people you hired. You need to establish a rhythm around consistent meetings and communication that involves a cascading trend that enables communication to flow through the entire organization. In our case, I get our leadership team together weekly. Important messages and key action items get cascaded down throughout the entire company as these leaders huddle up with their teams routinely. Most team leaders have structured meetings daily with their team members. Creating a daily, weekly, monthly, quarterly, and annual rhythm as it relates to meeting and communicating with the entire organization is critical to accomplishing personal, departmental, and company goals.

After reading books such as Verne Harnish's *Scaling Up* and many others, I realized that if I wanted to scale PFSbrands, I needed to turn my thought process upside down. How do we have productive meetings? What is the purpose of those meetings? What do productive meetings even look like?

The other major adjustment was to really nail down our key performance indicators (KPIs). What are the absolute, essential numbers that drive the business? What are the daily, weekly, monthly, and annual numbers that are most important to track? That took quite some time and the effort of several people to figure out. We threw out some of the numbers, those that we realized we didn't need to track, and identified the critical numbers that we did need to closely monitor on a daily, weekly, and monthly basis. Over the years, we've streamlined our KPIs and we consistently work to find ways to make them more visible to everyone. Keeping Score in business is essential to growing your revenue and creating a highly engaged team of winners.

So we started implementing our own huddles and zeroing in on our KPIs. We started having weekly huddles with all individuals who were assigned a general ledger code and I started getting my senior leadership team (SLT) together every week, same time, same agenda. We worked to keep structure in the meetings and to go through our numbers quickly while minimizing discussion of the KPIs till afterward. Depending on the people involved, each meeting had a slightly different rhythm. In our SLT weekly meeting, we looked at our most important KPIs and financial metrics. We were essentially just reporting and recognizing what the numbers revealed, and then the last hour was set aside for discussing and solving issues. Over the years, we've become accustomed to not being afraid to consistently look for ways to improve our meetings. Today, we always make sure that we have key action items from a meeting, identify who is assigned to those key action items, and decide the due date on the deliverable. We even ask every SLT member to grade each meeting on a scale of zero to ten, and we track the results over time. If someone rates the meeting low, I typically ask that individual to explain why it was rated it this way and what we can do to improve. Then we come back the next week, make sure we were able to check our action items off the list, and do it again. That's setting a rhythm and Keeping Score.

Because of my past disdain for meetings, and because I believe everyone's time is valuable, I have become a good moderator in our meetings and huddles. I also realize that my straight talk approach may intimidate some people from speaking up. If you want to conduct good meetings, you can't be afraid to speak up and say, "Hey, we're off track," or, "We're in the weeds. We can take this offline, one-on-one. We're wasting everybody else's time here." Over the years, people have come to know that if they have something to say, say it. Get to the point and don't ramble, because you'll get called out. At PFSbrands, in every conference room we have instructions for how to conduct efficient meetings.

pfs brands.	TIPS FOR RUNNING	
	EFFECTIVE MEETINGS	
(24) **Email an agenda** 24 hours in advance	Arrive **5 minutes** early	Start & end **on time**
NO Smartphones	Share all **relevant data**	Bring **paper & a pen**
Come **prepared**		
Disagree without being **disagreeable**		
Stay **on topic**	**Everyone** participates	**NO** interrupting
	Challenge ideas rather than people	Say it **ONCE,** any more is **POLITICKING**
Be brief and **concise**	**Follow up** by email within 24 hours	
Silence = **agreement**	**NO** side conversations or comments	
Always have an **agenda:**	1) Who needs to be present? 2) What are we talking about? 3) What do we need to achieve before we adjourn?	

The importance of effective meetings and communication jumps tenfold when you're an Open-Book Management company, because you're trying to share as much information as possible, you're trying to get all employees highly engaged, and ultimately your leaders must become educators, not managers. We believe that if we have to manage people, we've hired the wrong individuals. We want every single employee to be educated to the point where they can think and act like owners.

For me, understanding the communication component of establishing an organizational rhythm set in motion a complete 180-degree shift from being adamantly opposed to meetings to seeing how critical they are to scaling the business.

GOAL SETTING 101

Do you make a habit of setting goals? What's your process? How many of those goals have you actually written down? How often do you review your goals and check your progress? Did you know that people with written goals are 50 percent more likely to achieve them than people without written goals?[4] A Harvard study suggests 83 percent of the US population do not even have goals. That means, if you make a habit of setting goals, you can be in the top 17 percent of the US population, which offers you a distinct competitive advantage in becoming more successful in your life.

> People with written goals are 50 percent more likely to achieve them than people without written goals.

Of the 17 percent of people mentioned above, most of them do not write their goals down; they simply try to remember their goals in their heads. In other words, they think about something they would like to accomplish, never tell anyone, and never create a tracking mechanism to help them in achieving the goal. Obviously, you can't

---

4   "18 Facts about Goals and Their Achievement," GoalBand, accessed April 8, 2019, www.goalband.co.uk/goal-achievement-facts.html.

keep something in the front of your mind if you're not reminded of it more frequently.

I firmly believe that writing down goals is the first step in turning the invisible into the visible. But the reality is that only three out of every one hundred adults actually write down their goals.[5] So if 17 percent of the people in the US set goals and only 3 percent of those people write their goals down, the math would indicate that only 0.5 percent of the US population are setting goals AND writing their goals down. Do you find yourself a part of the other 99.5 percent? If so, don't feel too badly. Most people and most businesses fail to properly set and convey their goals.

In fact, the Harris Poll recently surveyed more than twenty-three thousand employees and found the following statistics:

- Only 37 percent of employees clearly knew their company's goals

- Only 20 percent were enthusiastic about these goals

- Only 20 percent could see how they could support these goals

- Only 15 percent felt like they were enabled to work toward those goals

- Only 20 percent fully trusted the company they worked for

Both personally and professionally, setting goals is crucial to success. In fact, we find it so important at PFSbrands that we've developed a required course for our team members: Goal Setting 101. We look to recruit and coach people who want to be more successful and we help them to get there by providing education on best practices for goal setting.

Here's an example of one employee-owner who has embraced

---

5   Ibid.

our goal setting mentality:

Kayci Cedars works for PFSbrands as a business advisor in Louisiana. Recently, she posted this on Facebook and gave me permission to include it in this book:

ONE YEAR is all that separates these two pictures [pictures not shown in this book]. *And while it might seem like I look better on the left, that is so far from the truth. This time last year I was SUFFERING from anxiety depression, stress, panic attacks, etc. I LET FEAR run my world. Those that were closest to me had zero idea how bad I was struggling because I went into overdrive to make sure no one knew the internal battle that I was dealing with.*

ONE YEAR AGO TODAY I went into a job interview that would change my life. I remember I had never been so nervous in the entirety of my existence. But the whole way there I prayed for this to be my breakthrough. I sang "Give Me Faith" by Elevation Worship at the top of my lungs. And I went into that interview and I crushed it. So much so that afterwards my now boss asked me if I was aware that I was interviewing with the CEO/President [I was one of the people interviewing Kayci that day] *of our company. God removed my fear. God filled me with confidence and hope.*

You see, one year ago if it wasn't for work, I didn't leave my house. I wouldn't even go to the gym because an elevated heart rate freaked me out. I let fear control every move I made.

After losing my dad I lost a couple more chunks of my heart. I didn't grieve. I kept pushing myself forward. I URGE you to grieve—because even if you're superwoman you have to slow down. You have to be gentle on yourself. Anxiety and fear only controlled me for a couple months, but those months were some of the darkest and scariest moments of my entire life I wouldn't wish that on anyone.

If you're letting fear control your life, I just want you to know that better days are ahead. Quit feeding your fear and keep moving forward. I don't even recognize the person I was a year ago. I look back and laugh at how silly it all seems. I don't hide behind a picture-perfect life on social media. I don't cake on makeup to make myself feel like I look better. I've learned it's much more important to work on what's going on inside. And I truly feel set free.

I felt compelled to send Kayci a personal note because I know people who have struggled with these issues. In fact, if I was a child in today's world, I would have likely been diagnosed with some type of anxiety issue. I had a speech problem as a child that caused me to be a little introverted and I avoided talking whenever possible. Luckily, I found sports as an outlet where I could lead by example, versus having to talk a lot.

As I read Kayci's post, something hit me. I believe my anxiety as a child, and even as a young adult, may be one of the reasons for my work ethic.

I reached out to Kayci with a personal email. Without sharing my email to her, this is part of her response back to me:

While the absence of my father is great, I have been blessed with some really good mentors who help me through these tough times. You are absolutely included in that. In fact, I haven't told you this yet but you inspired me to start working out. Today makes forty-two days (my original goal was twenty-one days, but I just keep going every day) in a row that I have made it to the gym and I'm down twenty pounds! So thank you for inspiring me! I am confident that my dad would and does approve of my path with PFSbrands thus far.

Kayci has come on board with PFSbrands and done a fantastic job as a business advisor. She may not have had the experience of other candidates, but we (the interviewing panel) picked up on her positive attitude and desire to improve. Success stories like this are why I'm so passionate about goal setting.

Goal setting, I mean serious goal setting, changes people's lives.

> The first step in understanding the importance of goal setting is to understand the *why*. If you don't set goals, write them down, and work to improve, you'll likely be the exact same person twelve months from now.

The first step in understanding the importance of goal setting is to understand the *why*. If you don't set goals, write them down, and work to improve, you'll likely be the exact same person twelve months from now. There's nothing necessarily wrong with that. Being who you are is okay, but the question is, Are you content with being the same … or do you want to be better, like Kayci?

This philosophy goes along very well with some of the things that I talk about in our core value sessions. Being okay with the status quo doesn't make you a bad person. But at the end of the day, if you're not working toward continuous improvement in a high-growth company, at some point the company will outgrow you. Take our warehouse, for example. In the early days, and even up until recently, our products and equipment items were picked by manual processes.

As we continued to scale, and due to various government requirements, it became necessary to implement a warehouse management system and introduce new technologies. If a warehouse worker is content with the manual processes and unwilling to change as the company grows, the employee-employer relationship is simply not a good fit anymore. It doesn't mean the individual is a bad person and it doesn't mean the company is a bad company; it's just not a good fit anymore. If you are a leader in a growing company, one of your most important roles is to consistently improve your team. In order to do this you have to recognize those team members who want to grow and those who don't. Those who do not want to grow need to be encouraged to find employment elsewhere, ideally with a company that is content with the status quo.

Goal setting allows you to see something in the future and break it down into more manageable, actionable pieces. You're able to forecast where you're going and how you'll get there. As you set goals, a word of CAUTION—don't focus on how you're going to reach those goals; just set them and trust in the incremental process of taking one step at a time. NEVER, NEVER, NEVER think about the path or the "how to" when you're in the goal setting stage. The path will present itself later as you break down your action steps. If you think about the "how" too soon, you will have too much self-doubt. I literally hate the word "can't." Whenever someone tells me that I can't do something, or that they can't do something, my blood pressure goes off the charts. After all, *I can't* really means *I won't*. I live in a world of positivity and I believe that anyone CAN accomplish anything that they want to as long as they can dream it and develop the GRITT to accomplish it.

WHAT'S A GOOD PROCESS?

First, know that effective goal setting takes time. Like most things in life, it takes practice and persistence to get good at it. And if you're new at goal setting, don't write a list of twenty things down, especially if you are working on your shorter-term goals. With longer-term goals, you can definitely have a bigger bucket list because you have time on your side. But if you want to accomplish short-term goals, a smaller list is better.

I personally like to set my goals annually. I spend a lot of time in November and December of each year working to determine what my short- and long-term goals are going to be for the year ahead. If you are new to goal setting and want to set some annual goals, start with a list of five to ten goals at the most. If you are new to goal setting and want to set some shorter-term goals (ninety days or less), three to five is a better recommendation. Digest your goals, then review them to make sure they are the right goals for you. Also make sure you set SMART goals: specific, motivational, attainable, relevant, and time based. Next, determine which ones are long term and which are short term. Put your short-term goals first and then your longer-term goals below them. After that, determine which of your goals are most important and place them in that order. Consider using an Excel spreadsheet if you want a simple way to sort and track your goals.

As you think about what you want to accomplish, don't be afraid to think big and believe you can achieve! An example is the four-minute mile. For years, people thought that the four-minute mile could never be achieved. Then on May 6, 1954, Roger Bannister, a junior doctor with minimal training, accomplished the feat in 3 minutes and 59.4 seconds.[6] Once the world saw it could be achieved, it only took forty-six days for someone else to run it faster.

After you decide what you want to accomplish next year, or even in the next ten years, it's always important to break down your action plans into smaller time periods. For a ten-year goal, what do you have to do each year to reach that goal? Then, what do you need to do each quarter to make that happen? How about monthly, weekly, and daily? The real secret to goal setting is to identify those key daily activities that need to take place in order to reach your goal. When you get good at doing this, you will become

> **The real secret to goal setting is to identify those key daily activities that need to take place in order to reach your goal.**

an all-star goal setter and someone who consistently outperforms 99.5 percent of your peers. In other words, you MUST identify those important activities that you need to do every day to get you to that goal. Next, you have to mentally COMMIT. I don't mean half-ass, I mean truly COMMIT to yourself and to others on what you plan to accomplish and what you plan to do each day to get there. Finally, you must create habits, systems, and processes that ensure you perform those daily habits. It's just like that old adage: How do you eat an elephant? One bite at a time.

---

6   "Roger Bannister," Wikipedia, accessed April 8, 2019, https://en.wikipedia.org/wiki/Roger_Bannister.

Most people want habits to be as easy as tying your shoes each day. Let's face it: greatness requires sacrifice. It requires doing what others won't do. Great habits are formed daily and they require consistent COMMITMENT. Highly successful people have learned to develop good habits. And when they get in a "rut," they have the GRITT to recommit and redevelop their best habits.

START, STOP, KEEP

One of the components we've incorporated in our Goal Setting 101 course is a concept adopted and adapted from *Scaling Up*: Start, Stop, Keep.

Start
What is a habit you could start that can help you achieve your goals? START doing.

Stop
What are you doing today that's preventing you from reaching your goals? STOP doing.

Keep
What can you do more of that is pushing you toward your goals? KEEP doing.

I personally believe the "Stop" question is far too often overlooked. So many people forget to focus on the things that they're doing that somebody else could do. For years I mowed my own grass. Even as our business was scaling and I was working sixty, seventy, or eighty hours a week, I was still mowing my own grass. My entire life at that time revolved around being able to get the grass cut. Finally, one day I asked myself, What am I doing that I shouldn't be doing?

What can I share that I really shouldn't be doing because it's not a productive use of time and energy for me and for the company? Guess what, I haven't mowed any grass in the last ten years. Something so simple, but yet it's such a huge burden removed from my weekly responsibilities that has allowed me more time with family and more time spent in other productive areas.

I've oftentimes made the mistake of hanging onto responsibilities far longer than necessary, everything from accounting, to email management, to sales management.

Handing the books off (the accounting side of the business) was one of the last major company responsibilities that I turned over to someone else. Despite the fact that I don't like accounting, I actually do love the numbers. Today, everyone knows I understand the numbers and I expect them to understand the numbers as well. However, looking back, I was doing all the month-end closing activities and preparing the financial statements myself, versus hiring the right person to handle these tasks. I just felt comfortable doing it since the work became a habit, and subsequently I held onto it probably four or five years longer than I should have.

This past year I've taken a big step in hiring someone to assist in handling my email traffic. To give someone complete visibility and access to your email is a big step. However, as a CEO I get a lot of internal and external emails that need attention, while also receiving an unbelievable amount of solicitation emails. Add an intense business travel schedule and it became nearly impossible for me to keep up with email management. Having someone to help prioritize, sort, filter, and assist with this email management has been another major step in allowing me to work ON the business rather than IN the business. I held off on this decision two or three years longer than I should have, but I'm pleased with the decision and with the person

I found to lead this effort. Not only has this person taken on email responsibility, but she also handles my calendar, project management, and note-taking and action items from all senior leadership team meetings, and she's been instrumental in helping to get this book finished. Along the way, she's become a good friend, an accountability partner, and someone to bounce ideas off of. Oh, and did I mention she didn't have any executive assistance experience when I hired her? Instead, what I saw in her was a great personality that meshes well with me, great organizational skills, great follow-up, past business experience, past sales experience, a positive attitude, and a desire to get better every day. Thanks, Lori K.

As another example of hanging on too long, I have to come back to yet another book that helped me to realize where I needed to improve. When I read Jack Daly's *Hyper Sales Growth* and *The Sales Playbook* several years ago, I realized that I was committing what Jack refers to as "one of the three sins of CEOs" who scale their business. I was buried with the responsibility of scaling the business and I was wearing the hat of both the CEO *and* the sales manager. Due to my passion for the business development side of our company, I was trying to do both jobs—and doing both of them half-assed.

As you probably know by now, I react quickly when I know what needs to be done, so immediately after reading the books I started planning for a new position of vice president of business development. I scheduled to attend one of Jack's workshops, which allowed me to meet him personally. This past year, my vice president of business development met with Jack and twelve other sales leaders three times as a peer group. By the way, I'm guilty of the other two CEO sins as well, so read *Hyper Sales Growth* if you want to know what those are.

Even though I had to let go of our vice president of business development recently, it was the right move to hire someone for this position. The move paved the way to a new corporate structure, allowing one of our seasoned leaders to be promoted to lead the business development team. As a leader, you're not always going to get it right. You're not always going to make the right decisions, nor is your team. Have a tolerance of failure and adjust as you go. In a start-up company, you oftentimes have to build the airplane as you fly. In a high-growth company, you must constantly look for ways to go higher and faster.

As every owner or entrepreneur grows their company, if they truly want to scale, they should constantly be looking at what they can offload in order to really focus on the things that drive the business. If you

> **If you want to grow your business, then you need to constantly find ways to work *on* the business instead of *in* the business.**

want to grow your business, then you need to constantly find ways to work *on* the business instead of *in* the business. The bottom line: you will not scale your company if you don't consistently ask the question, "What do I need to stop doing?"

STRATEGIES FOR BECOMING A GOAL GURU

DON'T JUST CREATE BUSINESS AND CAREER GOALS. Going back to our core purpose, we want to help people become more successful in work and in life. Use this goal-setting process to set personal goals for yourself. This is a great way to improve your own life and the lives of those around you. Find goals that drive you and that are compelling.

CREATE A BUCKET LIST. This isn't necessarily thought of

as goals by everyone, but you should create a list of things you want to do each year, and ultimately in your life. Just don't keep it to yourself. Jack Daly's bucket list for himself is completely out there for everybody to see on the internet. I encourage all of our employees to share their personal goals and bucket list with their leaders. If you don't tell us what you want to do personally, then we don't know what we don't know. Jack has great examples of people who have seen his bucket list and helped him to mark one of them off the list. One example is when someone said, "I see on your bucket list you wanted to play the top fifty golf courses in the world. I know somebody who knows somebody in Scotland at this particular course. I'll take care of one of those for you." If your goals are visible, you never know when someone may help you reach one.

HAVE BIG GOALS DUE AT DIFFERENT TIMES OF THE YEAR. You don't want to be in a position of trying to process all of your big goals at the same time. Be sure to prioritize these big goals during various times of the year so you can create more focus on them.

DON'T LISTEN TO NAYSAYERS. As I mentioned above, I get extremely frustrated with people who use the word "can't." Successful people learn to block these people out, and in most cases they separate themselves from these people all together. Real success requires that you set goals and have the GRITT to keep going despite all the negativity around you.

GET CREATIVE TO KEEP YOUR GOALS IN FOCUS. What are some creative ways to keep your goals top of mind? If you really want to accomplish your goals, create a system or find a way to make sure your goals are visible to you each day. I've seen some creative approaches here like physically writing goals on a mirror they look at every day. I've known people who have created "vision boards" with pictures of things they want to accomplish. The simplest approach is to keep a notepad by your bed or with you each day and ensure that you look at it each day.

WORK TOWARD ACHIEVING 70 TO 80 PERCENT OF YOUR GOALS. This may surprise a lot of you. Why not 100 percent? Because if you're consistently hitting 100 percent of your goals, then you're not setting them high enough. You're underperforming, you're not pushing yourself, you're not achieving maximum potential if you're hitting 100 percent of your goals day in and day out. Take a look at a great hitter in Major League Baseball. He's a superstar with a .300 batting average. That means he's getting out seven out of ten times he steps up to the plate. The point, however, is not that he gets on base three out of ten times, but that he doesn't get on base seven times. Success is a result of failure. It takes habit, GRITT, and practice.

BUILD AN ACCOUNTABILITY SYSTEM. Basically, create a network of people to hold you accountable. For example, say you want to get up and work out at 6:00 a.m. every morning. The absolute best way to ensure that it happens is to have ONE other person arrange to work out with you each morning. Why just ONE person? Because if you have a group of people it's easy to back out and not make the workout. However, if you have ONE person who's counting on you to be at the workout, think of how much peer pressure that puts on you to go. If you don't show up, you let them down.

Think of your goal-setting strategy like a three-legged bar stool. You need all three legs of the bar stool to successfully sit on the stool. When setting goals, first you need to establish those goals. Second, you need to write them down. Finally, if you really want to take it to the top level and be great at goal setting, then you must create a way to hold yourself accountable.

We build accountability into our goal setting at PFSbrands and we track everyone's goals with our self-developed system called GRITTrac. Everyone has full visibility of company goals, team goals, and professional goals, and each one of those are tied to each other.

> "I'll try" is not good enough, because it builds an unspoken but present excuse: "I TRIED."

And we accept no less than "I WILL" as a commitment. "I'll try" is not good enough, because it builds an unspoken but present excuse: "I TRIED." So personally, and in our organization with a tolerance of failure, we begin with "I will" and we use the "failures" to grow and recommit to "I will."

At PFSbrands, we support and expect nothing less than TRUE GRITT.

STEP UP TO THE PLATE
Turning Ideas into Action

I never thought of myself as a guy who believed in systems, processes, and rhythm. However, my entire life has revolved around setting big goals and working to achieve those goals. While I wasn't laser focused on creating the systems, processes, and rhythm early in my life, there was never an internal doubt in my ability to achieve anything I set my mind to. As I reflect back, knowing what I know now, I actually DID believe in systems, processes, and rhythm. I was mentally tough and diligent about how I went about achieving my goals in MY OWN life; I simply wasn't communicating this methodology with others. I wasn't "sharing the vision" and creating the expectations for others to follow.

Reading and learning from some of the best thought leaders in the world helped me to fine-tune my own systems, processes, and rhythms. By getting these systems, processes, and rhythms in writing and developing tools around them, I greatly enhanced my ability to be more successful, while providing others a way to become more successful in their own lives. By providing a framework for others to use, while also hiring servant leaders who believe in helping others excel, PFSbrands has been able to make a significant impact on others.

It's rewarding to know the impact I've had on other individuals. However, what's really powerful is to see these individuals taking these tools and passing along the ideas to others. Having others "pay it forward" allows us to reach many more people. As this trend continues, it will allow more people to excel and will undoubtedly help to rid the world of an entitlement mentality.

Questions to consider:

1. Do you currently have a meeting rhythm in your business?

2. Do you follow a structured process for goal setting for both you and your team members?

3. What do you need to start, stop, and keep doing in your business right now?

4. What is one position right now that if you added it today would make a positive impact on the top and bottom lines?

5. Are you ready to change your life? Set goals, write them down, and find an accountability partner. Mentally COMMIT to the daily activities necessary to accomplish your goals.

Shawn (in the cap) with his dad, Frank, and childhood friend, Mike Lamb.

Shawn applying labels on boxes for the first store opening in 1999.

One of the first Champs Chicken counters.

Models of the airplanes Shawn has owned.

A tribute to Shawn's favorite team and game:
Cardinals World Series Final Game in 2006.

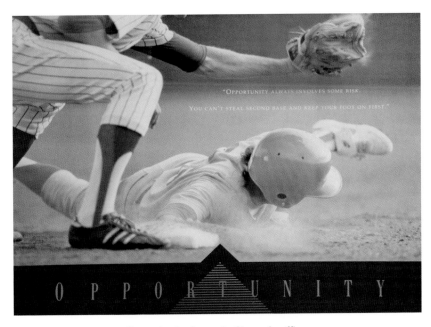

Opportunity frame in Shawn's office.

Shawn and his family at the twentieth anniversary celebration.

Shawn and his wife, Julie, at the twentieth anniversary celebration.

PFSbrands employee owners at the twentieth anniversary celebration.

Shawn and his family at the new headquarters building in 2018.

Shawn doing what he loves: flying.

Shawn's Cessna M2.

Shawn and some of the PFSbrands team flying to an event in 2019.

Shawn and Jack Daly.

Shawn and the Champs Chicken mascot.

Shawn at the opening of the first BluTaco stand-alone restaurant
in Holts Summit, Missouri, in 2019.

CHAPTER 7

True GRITT: Game-Winning Mind-Sets That Deliver Every Time

I had failed on an epic scale. An exceptionally
short-lived marriage had imploded... and
the fears of my parents, and those I'd had for
myself, had both come to pass. By every usual
standard, I was the biggest failure I knew.

J.K. ROWLING

There once was a man who wanted to become a great leader. At about every step he took, however, it seemed the road was paved with failures and setbacks. As he started out to make a name for himself in the state legislature, he suddenly lost his job, and ultimately lost the election. He picked himself up, dusted himself off, and decided to start a business. That, too, failed. Two years later, the woman he loved died unexpectedly, sending him into a nervous breakdown. Eventually, he recovered and went on to win a seat as a state representative. While in office, he tried to reach higher by running for the position as Speaker of the House but was defeated. A few years later he lost a bid to run for congress and not long after that was beat out in a race for the US senate. Even still he kept trying, the next time for vice president of the United States, and again, he lost. Despite the many failures and losses behind him, he still didn't give up, and in 1860 finally was elected as the sixteenth president of the United States. His name, if you haven't already guessed, was Abraham Lincoln. He persevered and succeeded when so many obstacles could have deterred him from continuing to pursue his dreams. But what was it that kept him going?

WHAT IS GRITT?

I've talked about it, I've dropped hints, I've probably made you think by now: *why does this guy keep spelling GRITT wrong?*

> It's that drive we have deep down to march onward toward our goals despite our exhaustion, our bruises, our failures, and the chatter around us, and often within us, that tells us we can't.

The truth is, GRITT couldn't be more right. In fact, as the title of the book suggests, you can't properly start Keeping Score *without* GRITT. We all know what *grit* is, right? Like in the story of President Lincoln, it's that intangible energy that keeps us going no matter the obstacles before us or behind us. It's that drive we have deep down to march onward toward our goals despite our exhaustion, our bruises, our failures, and the chatter around us, and often within us, that tells us we can't.

I know about that kind of grit all too well. As I mentioned, I grew up in a hardworking family, and was always encouraged to pursue my dreams. I've built a successful multimillion-dollar food-service company; launched and still own several other companies, including a business coaching company; became an author; and regularly speak at conferences, where, despite my speaking challenges as a kid, I typically receive positive feedback on my presentations:

"Great session and content! Have this speaker back again!"

"Shawn was very relatable and full of pertinent, useful information. He was captive, positive, and easy to listen to."

"Was very prepared, well spoken, and stayed on track. Did a great job of sharing the vision and execution of PFSbrands."

"Shawn did a really great job. He is down to earth and gets points across efficiently."

I share these comments not to brag or to highlight my prowess as a public speaker, but to illustrate how far I've come. Nearly everyone reading this book who knows me will be shocked by the fact that I couldn't talk very well as a kid. In fact, my sister, Michele, had to translate for me when I was an infant. I guess I had some hearing problems early on in life. It's not a vivid memory for me, but when my parents eventually discovered what was likely the root of the problem, doctors told me that I was only hearing about 50 percent of what most people hear. When I got tubes in my ears around age eight, I remember coming out of the hospital thinking that the cars going by on the local road sounded like jets. It was amazing how much of the world I had not been hearing. I went through speech therapy well into elementary school, just so I could try to learn to talk so people could understand me. As you might expect, I hated reading, writing, and getting up in front of people. When I read, I couldn't really concentrate. I would read a page in a book and have no idea what I had just read. I don't really know what caused this. In today's world where everyone wants to have answers, I may have been diagnosed with attention deficit disorder. Who knows? As a kid I justified my lack of desire to read with the reality that I'd rather be outside on a ball field or competing at something that allowed me to be active.

Being raised in the Catholic church and going through a private Catholic school until ninth grade, I had to get up at the lectern in church and read in front of people regularly. I wasn't a good reader because I didn't read much and, as I mentioned, I certainly wasn't a good speaker. That made it even tougher to get up in front of people and read out loud. While it was uncomfortable at the time, it forced me to do some of the things that ultimately have become a passion, from reading and writing to speaking publicly. With my southern accent, there may still be some people who say I didn't learn to talk.

> **At the end of the day, a lot of things happen to us throughout life. Unpredictable things. Unplanned things. But our grit is what can help see us through.**

At the end of the day, a lot of things happen to us throughout life. Unpredictable things. Unplanned things. But our grit is what can help see us through. In one of my favorite books, *Grit*, Angela Duckworth affirms this eloquently:

> *Grit grows as we figure out our life philosophy, learn to dust ourselves off after rejection and disappointment, and learn to tell the difference between low-level goals that should be abandoned quickly and higher-level goals that demand more tenacity. The maturation story is that we develop the capacity for long-term passion and perseverance as we get older.[7]*

---

[7] Angela Duckworth, *Grit: The Power of Passion and Perseverance* (New York: Scribner, 2016).

Angela has done a tremendous amount of research on grit in children and adults. She believes, and I agree with her, that grit is the main differentiator between those who are most successful and those who are not. I believe that 90 percent of success is just showing up regularly and getting "in the game." The rest of success involves the grit and persistence to always become better and work every day toward continuous improvement.

I actually gave Angela's book to my oldest daughter, Claudia, who thoroughly enjoyed it. Claudia inherited my poor hearing and speech problems. She had to have multiple sets of tubes and needed an even more complicated procedure to fix her ear drum. As a parent, I naturally thought at the time that this was all unfortunate. However, as I've seen Claudia mature over the years, I look back to her early childhood and wonder if these challenges didn't help her to establish the grit and determination she has today at the age of twenty-one. She is definitely goal driven, she's learned from her failures, and she has had to work harder than most young women her age. Claudia is generally a leader and seldom a follower. It will be interesting to see how her grit impacts her life.

TRUE GRITT

So now that we know what *grit* is, what is GRITT? Think of GRITT as *grit* 2.0. It's a culture, a philosophy, a method, and I've even pioneered a computer application called GRITTrac to help companies and individuals Keep Score. GRITT is actually an acronym I developed to help others work toward a mind-set of goal setting, accountability, and persistence:

G: Goal driven

R: Responsible

I: Involved

T: Team

T: Tolerance for failure

Take the Wright brothers, for instance. Their determination and persistence to build the world's first engine-powered, pilot-controlled aircraft captures every one of those concepts. But they wouldn't have had success at all if it wasn't for their repeated failures. It took the self-taught engineers years and numerous attempts to get anywhere close to powered flight. Dr. Jakab, a historian of technology and author of two books on the brothers said, "The Wrights saw the airplane as a system. It was not one invention, but many, and they all had to work in concert."

They planned and built their prototypes off of those who had tried and failed before them. And at the time, there were multiple different people working on some type of flying aircraft, some with a lot more financial backing behind them. Ultimately, however, the Wright brothers had the passion, the teamwork, the tolerance for failure, and the assumption of responsibility and were actively involved enough to see their dream become a reality. As *New York Times* writer John Noble Wilford puts it about that significant moment in aviation history:

> *There, near the fishing village of Kitty Hawk, they set up camp at Kill Devil Hills. On a blustery Thursday morning, Orville and then Wilbur, then Orville and Wilbur again, made four flights. Their two-winged craft took off from a 60-foot wooden launching rail, headed against a wind of more than 20 miles an hour. On the first test, Orville flew 120 feet in 12 seconds.*

The last and longest flight, by Wilbur, covered 852 feet in 59 seconds. Around noon that day, one of the few witnesses, young Johnny Moore, raced down the beach shouting, "They done it, they done it, damned if they ain't flew!"[8]

Now let's do a deeper dive into each letter in GRITT.

G: Goal Driven

To be goal driven, you have your eye on the prize at all times. You know exactly what you want to do, and every setback you experience only reinforces your tenacity to reach that goal.

One of my father's favorite baseball players was Cal Ripken Jr. He admired Cal's work ethic, class, and unbelievable determination toward a goal. Ripken began his run at immortality on May 30, 1982, determined to beat Lou Gehrig's streak of consecutive games played, a whopping 2,103 in a row. Now anyone who even remotely knows anything about Major League Baseball knows that injuries are commonplace.

Over the course of the next thirteen years, Ripken played hard to win each and every game as he worked toward his goal. He suffered numerous injuries—hit in the hand with a fastball while batting, nearly dislocating his shoulder while reaching for a catch, playing with a broken nose, and tearing his knee after a brutal crash while sliding for home, just to name a few. In fact, during Ripken's streak, other players made 5,045 trips to the disabled list.[9]

---

8   John Noble Wilford, "Earliest Days: Takeoff! How the Wright Brothers Did What No One Else Could," the *New York Times* archives, December 9, 2003, https://nyti.ms/2qXIBNN.

9   Peter Schmuck, "Streak of Fate: Ripken's Repeated Collisions with Adversity Show Fine Line He Has Tread for 1,887 Games," the *Baltimore Sun*, September 24, 1993, www.baltimoresun.com/sports/orioles/cal-ripken-jr/bal-streak-of-fate-ripken-s-repeated-collisions-with-adversity-show-fine-line-he-has-tread-for-1-887-gam-20150830-story.html.

"He has been fortunate to avoid serious injury, but he doesn't avoid injury," said Orioles manager Johnny Oates. "He's banged up like everybody else. He plays with pain and he plays well with pain, but if he gets hurt, he feels it like everybody else."[10]

"I try not to think about that," said a then-thirty-three-year-old Ripken. "If you play hard and concentrate all the time, that insulates you and protects you. When you're focused, you know that there's a chance somebody is going to run into you at second base and you're prepared for that. You don't take for granted that you are going to stand up at any base, so you never have to slide at the last minute. When you're not paying attention, that's when you can be caught off guard."[11]

He broke Gehrig's record in 1995, then went on to eventually end up with an incredible 2,632 consecutive games played.

If that's not goal driven, then I don't know what is.

R: Responsible

Responsible, for me, means a couple things. Number one, just being a responsible human being, you're responsible for your own actions toward your friends, family, neighbors, and coworkers. You take that responsibility seriously. You realize that *you* are responsible for the results related to your actions, whether those results are bad or good. In essence, taking responsibility is really about taking ownership and being accountable for your actions.

At an OBM company, the visibility of each person's responsibility is heightened. Everyone knows what everyone else is responsible for, when deliverables are due, what numbers need to be met. Everybody is working toward the same company goals. We give every

---

10   Ibid.

11   Ibid.

employee our company playbook, so everybody knows exactly what the company is trying to accomplish on a quarterly basis, an annual basis, and beyond. There's really no excuse for not knowing what the company objectives are.

At PFSbrands, each leader is responsible for getting with the individuals they lead, sitting down with them on a quarterly basis, and saying, "Okay, here are our company goals. It's our job to create departmental and individual goals that will help the company achieve these goals." Each employee helps to develop their departmental goals with their team, so it's not a downward command-and-control-type management system. It's a group effort to set these individual and company-wide goals.

In fact, we do company-wide surveys to collect the wisdom of the crowd each quarter. We give every single individual in the company an opportunity to tell us what they feel is most important for the company to accomplish in the coming quarter. We compile and organize all of this feedback and give it to our senior leadership team before they go on their offsite meetings at the end of each quarter. My senior leadership team and I look at all of the feedback and come to a decision on what we feel is most important for the upcoming quarter. We develop our company goals based upon what everyone feels is most important. Essentially, our people work to affect what they create. The theory of responsibility is if you get people involved in the goal-creation process, they are more likely to engage and take ownership.

> The theory of responsibility is if you get people involved in the goal-creation process, they are more likely to engage and take ownership.

I: Involved

If you want to develop and hone that growth mind-set, then you as an individual absolutely *must* be involved. We constantly talk with our leaders about the necessity of working to get their people involved. They must nurture that involvement with all team members.

This crosses over a bit into our hiring process. We actually have a career history form that potential new hires are required to fill out. This is not a short form and virtually every candidate we've ever interviewed has commented that they've never had to do anything like it. They've never had to fill out a form like it just to be considered for an interview. The career history form revolves around not only GRITT, but also our core values. We ask questions about the potential employee's personal habits, about personal goal setting. We want to know if they are driven, curious, or satisfied with the status quo. And we look for individuals who have a growth mind-set because we've had double-digit revenue growth since our inception and we plan to keep this track record. So you must have a growth mind-set to succeed at PFSbrands. If you're not competitive and not one to embrace change while being actively involved with your team, then you're really not going to be a fit here, because the fast pace will wear you out.

T: Team

Team really means nothing more than you've got to set the egos aside. Leaders are notoriously narcissistic and egotistical, and there is no greater threat to business than an ego in a team environment. There's a major difference between egotistical and confident. We look for servant-leaders who are confident and we look for individual contributors who work well within a team environment.

I was recently talking to one of our business developers who was visiting the corporate office from Indiana, a guy who has been with us almost a year at the time of this writing. He hadn't had a chance to visit our new offices yet, so he came in to Missouri for our Discovery Days and brought some prospective customers with him. Apparently, he had recently left a somewhat toxic work environment, and as we were talking he said, "I've just never worked at a place like this … where you don't see egos. The leadership team isn't worried about protecting their turf, or worried about somebody else outshining them. Everybody is focused on bringing up the whole ship."

It's not always about having the most talented players to make up a successful team. While I firmly believe in hiring A players, I also realize that the most successful teams are those that ultimately figure out how to encourage each and every player to work cohesively. In order to do that, you must put

> **The most successful teams are those that ultimately figure out how to encourage each and every player to work cohesively.**

the egos aside and know that decisions have to be made and all actions should be taken with the *team* in mind, not just the individual.

T: Tolerance for Failure

Here's why we have the second "T" in our GRITT model. Because of my mind-set, I was naive of the fact that there is such an overwhelming fear of failure in the world. It seems now more than ever people and business are ruled by this irrational fear. It dictates decisions, actions, and ultimately outcomes. Just imagine if people such as Abraham Lincoln, or the Wright brothers, or Thomas Edison had given up on their dreams because of the fear of failure. Edison said it best: "I have not failed. I've just found ten thousand ways that won't work."

Because of the zero-tolerance-for-failure mentality, people

have become afraid to try new things because they don't want to be punished. This fear of being punished absolutely kills innovations. Of course, this isn't to say that we want to be a failing company. We make it pretty well known that we like to win. But winning doesn't happen without a lot of failure. And we encourage people to set their goals higher while being willing to fail. We don't beat them up if they've set an aggressive goal and they don't hit it. As mentioned in the last chapter, my philosophy is if you're hitting 100 percent of your goals, then you haven't set them high enough. Aim for a 70 percent to 80 percent success rate, and you're probably setting your goals the way you should be.

Take the quote that opened this chapter by J. K. Rowling. I think it's worth reading a second time: "I had failed on an epic scale. An exceptionally short-lived marriage had imploded... and the fears of my parents, and those I'd had for myself, had both come to pass. By every usual standard, I was the biggest failure I knew."

Those are the words of the author whose Harry Potter book series has been translated into seventy-three languages, sold millions of copies, and accrued more than $20 billion through movie adaptations and sponsorships. My daughter Ali is an avid reader and a huge fan of the Harry Potter series. Ali's reading habit at such a young age has made her wise beyond her years. One night she told me about all of the adversity Rowling had gone through before achieving her goals— suffering from severe depression, contemplating suicide, dozens of rejections from publishers, living through an abusive marriage, the sudden loss of her mother to multiple sclerosis, and being a single mother struggling to pay the bills.

"Failure meant a stripping away of the inessential," said Rowling. "I stopped pretending to myself that I was anything other than what I was and began to direct all my energy into finishing the only work that mattered to me."[12]

I think back to how PFSbrands started as a coffee company. Essentially, we failed to make it. I could have quit right then and there. I could have said, "That's it, I'm just going to work for somebody else." But I kept going. Yet, was that my last failure? Not by a long shot.

At one point, a friend of mine named John Bleidistel was looking to do something on his own to get into business. We talked about it quite a bit and we both decided to partner up on a Champs Chicken location. This was technically going to be the first standalone Champs Chicken operation and we were opening it in the small town of California, Missouri. The location we leased was a former Taco Bell and had a drive-through and everything. Just perfect. We leased the space from the owner of the convenience store it was connected to, and we really decked it out. The food quality was good, of course, but in time we realized that the location just wasn't generating the daily volume necessary to make the business profitable. We were losing a couple thousand dollars a month. The gross margins were good, but we simply could not get the top-line sales to a level that would cover our overhead and payroll expenses. Like all businesses, there is a certain amount of revenue that you need to generate in order to make the business model work. We had to make the tough call and shut the business down.

Looking back, we passed up a different location with a much higher traffic count in Jefferson City that likely would have made all the difference between success and failure. The rent was nearly twice as high, but we should have taken that location. We just picked the wrong one.

---

12   J. K. Rowling, "The Fringe Benefits of Failure, and the Importance of Imagination," the *Harvard Gazette*, June 5, 2008, https://news.harvard.edu/gazette/story/2008/06/text-of-j-k-rowling-speech/.

Being an optimist and believing in a higher authority, I always believe things happen for a reason. When adversity hits, I look to persevere and look for ways to adjust. A really positive thing came out of this failure, as John Bleidistel ultimately ended up becoming an employee with PFSbrands, and has been with us for more than a decade. He is currently our director of technology and has turned out to be a great asset to the company. John also serves on our senior leadership team today.

And even as I write this we are working on another standalone unit. We certainly have a lot more knowledge now and we are not deterred by the fact that one standalone location didn't work. We'll just work more diligently to put this next one in a better location.

KEEPING SCORE WITH GRITT

As we were scaling PFSbrands, I realized we needed a way to more effectively and efficiently track all the moving parts of a high-growth, fast-paced company. I needed to get an omniscient view and expand on our culture of high visibility and high expectations. I am adamantly opposed to micromanaging. As I mentioned earlier, I don't even want to hire people who need to be managed. However, I fully support an environment where there is full accountability and visibility. I believe so much in our GRITT model at PFSbrands that we decided to make

> I believe so much in our GRITT model at PFSbrands that we decided to make the intangible *tangible* by creating the GRITTrac system.

the intangible *tangible* by creating the GRITTrac system. Initially, the system was designed for me as a CEO, so I could keep track of the entire set of company goals and how we are progressing toward them. The system has been designed to keep a running scoreboard in real time.

But I decided to take it a step further and use it to help us as a company keep score. With this innovative, user-friendly software, everyone in our company can log in and see our entire strategic plan, our company-wide key performance indicators, our annual goals, our quarterly goals, and much more. Not only that, every individual can see their team's goals and enter their own professional and personal goals. The GRITTrac system is designed to help individuals, leaders, and the CEO track all of these important things. Suddenly, everyone in the company is Keeping Score and following the action. Much like the rest of our company, we are continuously adding to and improving the GRITTrac system.

The GRITTrac system at its heart is really designed for every single individual to get into a GRITT mind-set—to create goals, to be responsible, to be involved with the company, to make sure they know where the team is, and to have that tolerance of failure. It's all about making sure every individual has complete visibility of the company goals, the strategic plan, our strengths and weaknesses. In fact, our entire strategic plan pops up right on the front page when you open up GRITTrac. Each and every day, every employee can see where they stand on all of their goals, where their team stands on their goal progress, and where the entire company stands on our quarter goals, the one-year goals, and the three-year goals. Each individual can clearly see how their goals affect the overall company goals. After all, it's proven that employees want to know how their contributions are affecting the company. GRITTrac provides that amazing visibility.

Think about a basketball game. When the coach calls a time-out, what is the first thing most of the players do? They look at the scoreboard to see what the score is, and to see how much time is left. No one would even think to put a player out there on a basketball court and not have a scoreboard.

But that's exactly what the majority of businesses out there do. They don't have a scoreboard up, and if they do, they have not shared the rules of the game. Most businesses don't teach their employees about financial literacy, and thus they don't even know how the hell to play the game.

To be highly successful in business, and in life, we must support and expect nothing less than true GRITT.

STEP UP TO THE PLATE
Turning Ideas into Action

When you talk to most successful people, especially those who started from nothing or dealt with adversity in their lives, you will commonly hear grit as one of key reasons they feel they've been successful. The ability to take risks, set big goals, and accept failures is common among successful individuals. However, those people who can continuously keep pushing themselves, those who can fail time and time again, and those who can "get up and dust themselves off" after each failure are the people who ultimately prove to be most successful.

The GRITT mentality talked about in this chapter is a starting point to help you prepare MENTALLY for what it takes to be successful. Regardless of how you define success as an individual, if you begin to change your mental approach to goal setting, you've positioned yourself for much greater success in your life.

ALWAYS start with "I WILL" and watch how your life changes.

Questions to consider:

1. Think back on the personal and professional goals that have gone unmet. Was the reason due to a lack of grit? Based on what you have learned in the previous pages, could those goals have been met?

2. Take a mental note of the company leaders in your organization and jot down the adversity that they have overcome in their lives. When you have a chance, thank them for staying the course. Consider doing this with other team members you work closely with.

3. How can you take the key points you have learned about grit and turn this into a coaching and mentoring opportunity in your company?

4. Are you doing everything possible to be INVOLVED at your company?

5. Be on the lookout for people who say "I'll try" and consider asking them to COMMIT with "I WILL." Do you catch yourself saying "I'll try"? If so, consciously work on taking "I'll try" out of your vocabulary and work on COMMITTING to actions.

CHAPTER 8

Topgrading to Win: How the Right Team Can Make All the Difference

People are not your most important asset. The right people are.

JIM COLLINS

W hen Madi Books interviewed with PFSbrands back in 2015, it didn't quite go as expected. Previously, she had worked for a couple of start-up companies that didn't pan out. But being in IT and specializing in data quality and reporting, she knew that finding work wouldn't be difficult. Yet Madi didn't necessarily want a job. She wanted a career.

That said, she was extremely selective in her process to find the right potential fit. During her initial interview at PFSbrands with our CFO, Trevor Monnig, she noticed we are very selective as well. Within the first five minutes, Trevor told Madi that the position he was trying to fill wasn't for her. Not because of anything she had said or done, but because we were specifically looking for a C# developer. But in her resume, he saw her experience with data quality and thought it would be a good idea to bring her in for a conversation around the subject—to better understand the concept of data quality as well as the pros of developing such a program.

"Well, I figured I was just going to keep talking, because by that point I didn't have anything to lose. There was a transition into more of a conversation than your traditional interview, and we just began learning about each other. It was really laid back, which made it easy to talk about my passion and learn what PFSbrands had to offer," said Madi, regarding the interview. She just relaxed and continued to engage with Trevor, explaining that she intended for the next place she landed to be the home for her career.

And then something unusual happened. At some point during that conversation, Madi and Trevor actually came to the conclusion that PFSbrands *did* need someone with her level of data quality knowledge and experience. Trevor came to me the next day and said that he had interviewed an intelligent young woman who could take our data processes to a whole new level. He called it "big data." He asked if I would be willing to interview Madi and consider creating a new position for her. Madi came in to interview with me on a Saturday morning and we ended up creating a position for her, realizing that we were a good fit for each other.

So she was hired in as an IT specialist and over time assumed the role of data manager—basically collecting, crunching, and reporting numbers. Madi stated, "It was a really unique process where I got to work directly with the senior leadership team. And throughout that process, I was able to gain insight into how straight talk and team-focused the culture at PFSbrands truly is."

However, a few years into her role, Madi started feeling like she just wasn't progressing professionally as she thought she should. She voiced her concerns to Trevor, and over a week-long process was tormented by not knowing if she should quit and move on. Then she decided as a last-ditch effort to dig into some of the books listed in our Better Book Club: *The No Complaining Rule,* by Jon Gordon; *The Sales Development Playbook,* by Trish Bertuzzi; and *Grit,* by Angela Duckworth, among others. As a marathon runner who trained often, and to feel twice as productive, she listened to the audiobooks instead of reading. What she realized was eye opening: it wasn't the job that was getting in the way of her happiness ... it was her attitude.

> **What she realized was eye-opening: it wasn't the job that was getting in the way of her happiness ... it was her attitude.**

"I started the process of self-evaluating and realized *I* was the source of the negativity. I think people try to separate their lives to create a work-life balance. As if your passions are one thing, and what you do for a living is another. I've learned that goal setting and trying to make my career a passion were key. My negativity had even spilled over into my personal life, to where I was complaining at home about things that quite honestly didn't need to be complained about. I didn't want to be that person who brought problems and complaints home. My husband was worried about me, about why I was unhappy. Yet all it took to change things was a shift in perspective."

The truth is, we knew all along that Madi was one of our many A players. Sometimes, all it takes is a little motivation and mentoring to bring out a team member's finest. Ultimately, when these A players are in a rut, they just need someone who cares to help them to determine the best course forward. Then, *they* make the decision to make their own course adjustments.

That's what Topgrading is all about.

TOPGRADING IS TEAM BUILDING

Just like a professional sports franchise looks to wins games by recruiting the best athletes, a company that wants to compete and succeed in any market needs to recruit the best employees.

Dr. Brad Smart, an industrial psychologist and leading expert in the science of talent acquisition and retention, coined the term "Topgrading" as the "practice of creating the highest quality workforce by ensuring that talent acquisition and talent management processes focus on identifying, hiring, promoting, and retaining high performers, A players, in the organization at every salary level."[13]

After devouring Smart's book of the same name, I knew we needed a change. Prior to reading *Topgrading*, we had a very loose hiring process. When we needed to fill a position, we conducted a few interviews, got a gut feeling, and if the potential hire seemed reasonably intelligent and capable, that was enough for us. Fortunately for me, I've always had an innate ability to read people and quickly assess their values. However, to take our company to the next level, we needed to create a system and process for recruiting, interviewing, hiring, and retaining people who not only fit the position, but ultimately fit the culture of PFSbrands.

It certainly wasn't perfect at first. It was a different thought process for the entire company, going from "filling a seat" to "filling a seat with the *right* person." We became dedicated to finding A players, then to coaching and keeping them. But just like with a smaller sports franchise, the reality is you may not yet have the resources to recruit a

---

13 "FAQs," Topgrading, accessed April 8, 2019, https://www.topgrading.com/.

Michael Jordan. Small- to midsize companies are not always going to be able to attract A players. Sometimes, you have to recruit B players who you can coach and refine into A players.

That's where Topgrading and Carla Dowden come in.

FROM A HUMAN RESOURCES DEPARTMENT TO A PEOPLE SUCCESS TEAM

Carla came to PFSbrands in 2010, when we had about thirty-five employees. We were connected through our kids, as our two oldest daughters played soccer together. At the time, her job with her current employer was being transitioned to Atlanta, Georgia. We didn't really need a full-time Human Resources director. In fact, we didn't have a senior leadership team and no real corporate structure to speak of. But when I shared the details about PFSbrands, particularly about our culture and my vision, her eyes lit up. I brought Carla on part-time and within thirty days she had made such a massive contribution to the company that I offered her a full-time position.

Carla says:

My intent was to come aboard and show Shawn that I could do more than just human resources (HR). I had come from a background of family business too. My dad owned a grocery store, and so having that entrepreneur background meant that I knew more than just HR. I understood operations, finances, and work ethic. And Shawn had a lot of great ideas about the mission, vision, and core values of the company ... but nothing was in writing.

He already had a very strong culture in place when I came on board. This was simply a result of his personal values and the way he treated people. But I knew to continue to grow that culture, it would be important to get all those things out of his head and on paper, so we could share that information with the team, and with potential hires and franchisees.

Carla understood that we can teach a lot of things to individuals, but if they don't fit the culture from the beginning, if they don't have the mind-set of wanting to be challenged every day, of wanting to be successful in what they do in work and in life, then we're doing a disservice to PFSbrands, and to the individual. We needed to start Keeping Score.

I'm adamantly opposed to employee reviews. I think they are worthless and just create a lot of tension and anxiety in the workplace. However, Keeping Score at PFSbrands has ultimately led us to eliminate our HR department and replace it with what we now call our people success department.

Our core purpose is to help others become more successful in work and in life. And it all starts with onboarding.

THE CAREER HISTORY FORM

Once a candidate submits a resume and possibly moves through a brief initial interview if we see potential, we have them fill out our career history form. This is a seven-page form that really gets to the nitty-gritty of what makes the person tick. Questions like: What does work life balance mean to you? What does work ethic mean to you? What motivates you? On a scale of one to ten, how competitive are you? How many times do you get to make a first impression?

ONBOARDING WITH STYLE

Carla has a sandbox on her desk. It's not filled with a true sand, but with that magnetic sand you can play with and shape. "Sometimes new hires might be a little nervous to come into my office," says Carla. "So it's a gadget that people can play with. But it also serves as a great visual. I tell them, 'I am very involved in this company. I have my heart and soul invested in this company. This is my passion. And I will play in everyone's sandbox.'" What Carla means is if she sees something that doesn't look right, or something that could be detrimental to the company as a whole but it's happening in the marketing department or in sales or in finance, she's going to voice her concerns.

And every single employee at PFSbrands is encouraged to do the same, because that's a critical element in Keeping Score.

When we onboard someone, we want to make it a great experience. They are welcomed by dozens of emails from their team members before even stepping foot on our property for their first day. We also send out a welcome package to their home with a copy of this book and some little trinkets about the company, like a cool cup, maybe a pen and notepad. It's not just a welcome package for the individual that we hired, but for the family as well, because they have now all become a part of the PFSbrands family.

We hold a brief presentation in one of our conference rooms to give a bit of history about the company, and to share a little about each department and its function. Then just like a new player stepping out on the court for a basketball game, a group of team members, anywhere from twenty-five to forty people, gathers outside that conference room to welcome the individual with a high five as they pass down the hall.

We not only hire, we *develop* people. When people truly embrace our culture, utilize our resources, and develop relationships with our leaders, they can learn far more than they could at any four-year university. That's a critical factor of our core purpose: to make others more successful in work and in life.

> We not only hire, we *develop* people. When people truly embrace our culture, utilize our resources, and develop relationships with our leaders, they can learn far more than they could at any four-year university.

We highly encourage people to share with us what their vision is and where they want to go professionally and personally. Why? Because that's what makes for success in work and in life. If we're able to help them to grow and accomplish some of those things, it makes them a better person and it makes PFSbrands a better company.

We hold people accountable. We care. We have fun, but we have high expectations. You have to like competitiveness. You have to like change and a fast-paced environment. You have to like having your performance be very visible. You have to be a person who commits to continuous personal and professional growth. To be successful here, you have to have that passion and drive to continuously improve what you're doing. People know early on that if you want to come in and do the status quo, PFSbrands is not the place for you ... because we will never settle. We're in continuous improvement mode, continuous learning. The culture at PFSbrands is not for everyone and we're looking for specific qualities in individuals as we go through our interview process.

For our team, it's all about gratitude. It's not, "I have to go to work today." It's, "I *get* to go to work today."

Every company has a culture. Your company culture can be created by accident or you can purposely focus on it. To purposely focus on your culture, you have to put the correct leadership team in place and ensure that they fully understand your expectations. Here are the expectations I have laid out for my senior leadership team.

SENIOR LEADERSHIP TEAM EXPECTATIONS AND PLEDGE

The overall function of the senior leadership team (SLT) is to drive PFSbrands's culture and strategy forward. While we all have to work *in* the business, their role is more of a function of working *on* the business. These individuals are not solely focused in their own area but have a cross-departmental view and have a more strategic mind-set.

The vision of the PFSbrands SLT is to be no larger than eight people in total. This team should have diversity and contain individuals from various departments and/or divisions of the company.

The following is a list of expectations and commitments needed to serve on our SLT. Serving PFSbrands at this level is a distinct honor and comes with a great deal of accountability. Understand that this team can and will change as we grow. Some of our SLT members may be asked to step down and take on other roles. If this happens, keep in mind that it doesn't mean your opinion and expertise are not valued.

Below are the expectations and your pledge as an SLT member:

1. **COMMITMENT:** Treat the role of team member as seriously as your individual leadership role.

2. **TRANSPARENCY:** If it affects more than one of us, put it on the team table.

3. **PARTICIPATION:** Each member's voice is welcomed on issues affecting the enterprise.

4. **INTEGRITY:** What you say and do when you are with the team is what you say and do when you are outside the team.

5. **BUILD TRUST:** Defending others even when they are not present, honoring commitments, keeping no secrets, welcoming others' interest and questions about your area (no protecting one's turf), collaborating, and developing others.

6. **DON'T CUT SOMEONE OFF AT THE KNEES TO MAKE YOURSELF LOOK TALLER:** Attack the issues, not the person. Work through appropriate channels and be conscious of what your fellow leaders (SLT and leaders at all levels) are trying to accomplish.

7. **BE DECISIVE:** Take measured risks, be innovative, admit mistakes, and take a stand on issues.

8. **BE ACCOUNTABLE:** See it. Own it. Fix it.

9. **READ OR LISTEN TO** at least twelve books per year and log them in the Better Book Club.

10. **HOLD GREAT MEETINGS:** Well-planned with agendas, start and end on time, no sidebar conversations, and create next steps and accountabilities at meeting's close.

11. **DELIVER RESULTS:** Deliver on commitments with "iron will determination to make it happen."

12. **THE LEADER LEADS:** I will decide when a decision will be made by 100 percent agreement, by majority, or by me. I expect you to run your teams accordingly.

13. **BE WILLING TO STEP DOWN** from the SLT if asked to do so and be willing to continue serving the company at a high level.

14. **A DECISION IS A DECISION:** Once a decision has been made, each member will support it as the team's decision. We will not continually reopen decisions made. Passive disagreement is not an option.

15. **AMBASSADORS:** One voice will come out of our meetings. Each of us will speak for the whole team. We will all live by our five guiding principles and the Happiness Rule.

16. **HAVE FUN:** Life is short.

COACH YOUR PEOPLE UP, OR COACH YOUR PEOPLE OUT

We recently had our twenty-year anniversary as of this writing. We've shown a nineteen-year track record of double-digit growth and been recognized by Inc. as one of the fastest-growing privately held companies in the United States for nine years in a row. Only .04 percent of the Inc. 5000 winners can claim the same thing. Honestly, if I had known about the Inc. 5000 list before the first time applying for the honor, our company would likely have a fifteen-year track record on the prestigious list. Our entire team is proud of this accomplishment, and, trust me, it takes an entire team of dedicated people to make this happen.

Yet rapidly growing companies and companies that consistently scale year over year are faced with a unique challenge. As a leader in a growing company, you have to recognize this challenge and be willing to address it.

Growing companies must have a learning culture. The leaders as well as all employees must have a continuous improvement mind-set and be willing to consistently learn new skills. Everyone must be willing to learn at a pace consistent with the company's growth. They must be willing to adapt to the changes occurring, which include new talent being added, culture changing, organizational changes, turnover, and much more.

As the founder of PFSbrands, I've lived all of these changes. My role has consistently changed over the years and it will continue to change as we experience more growth. I've challenged myself to learn something new every day. I've surrounded myself with awesome leaders, coaches, and mentors who challenge me and hold me accountable. I've consistently set my goals high, and I wake up every day with a positive attitude and a belief that these goals can be achieved.

One of the most frustrating things for any coach (and I've always viewed my role as a coaching position) is to have individuals who can't seem to "make the leap." In other words, these are great people who simply can't change their ways to continue to fit within the organization as it grows. They either can't look in the mirror and see their weaknesses that need to be corrected, or they simply don't want to put in the effort to correct those weaknesses.

Many individuals have a "ceiling" on their capabilities. At PFSbrands, we've continuously improved our hiring processes, and we usually hire individuals with a skill set that enables them to scale with us. However, occasionally we still have individuals that are challenged to "make the leap." We work diligently with these individuals to find them a role on our team in which they can excel. When corrections need to be made, we sit down and have honest conversations with them about what needs to be improved upon. We provide them every opportunity and every tool we can to help them adapt. We do everything possible to "coach them up."

In and of itself, this is more than most companies will do. It's a lot of effort to sit down routinely with every employee and have conversations about their career path. However, the companies that are truly able to scale year over year take it a step further.

The companies that are able to scale up consistently have a unique mind-set. For those people who ultimately can't "make the leap," you have to "coach them out."

> For those people who ultimately can't "make the leap," you have to "coach them out."

You have to help these individuals realize that your company is no longer the best fit for them. Ultimately, when you have an established company culture in which the majority of employees work with the same mind-set, it becomes a team effort to constantly work to help "coach out" those individuals who are no longer a great fit. If you truly want to establish a culture of winning and growing, then you must always be working to ensure that you have the best possible talent on the team. When someone leaves the team, you work to replace them with a better player.

You may be asking, "What happens if they don't get it?" or, "What happens if you can't coach them out?"

That's where most leaders fail. Most leaders can't make the tough decision that is necessary. There's only one thing left that you can do. You have to let this person go, regardless of how long they have been with the company and what contributions they've made to the company. If they don't fit culturally or if they are not performing in their role, then you have to let them go. While these are tough conversations, if you've done everything you can to help them along the way and if you've done everything you can to communicate expectations, then you are justified in making this decision.

Here are three tips from my experience:

1. Work to help the person find another job or allow them some time to find another job if they are a good person. In most cases, these people that don't "make the leap" are still great people; they are just no longer a fit for your organization.

2. When firing someone is done correctly (and I've not always done it correctly), most people feel relieved and have an element of respect for you. I try to never make it personal, but focus on the lack of results or talk about the fact that the individual is just not fitting in with our culture. In my case, I've been able to hold on to a positive relationship in about 90 percent of the cases. Most of the other 10 percent never would take accountability for their actions. They could not "look in the mirror" and realize that it was their fault they were not producing appropriate results or not working to fit in with the team. In one particular case early in my business's life cycle, I simply screwed up and didn't handle the firing correctly. Even though I made the right decision, I wish I had that one back to better handle the departure.

Generally, when you finally make a move to responsibly offboard someone, the rest of the team wonders what took you so long.

The day after the person is gone, you feel a sense of "relief" at having the issue behind you, and now have the ability to focus your effort on productive tasks that help to grow your business. In a couple of instances, I have received a thank-you note a few weeks later for doing the terminated employee a favor.

In all cases, I've been able to replace the person with a more-solid contributor who better fit the culture. In many cases, we recruited a person with a much different skill set that better met the needs of the company at that time.

3. If you want to scale your business, focus on helping your employees to become more successful. In the process, be mindful of their ability to work within a growing team that has a lot of changes happening. Most important, if you are the leader of a company, be willing to have the tough conversations and make the tough decisions. Don't delegate this responsibility and don't count on your inexperienced leaders to make these tough decisions.

> **If you are the leader of a company, be willing to have the tough conversations and make the tough decisions.**

As a leader, it's YOUR job to "coach your people up, or coach your people out."

If you don't, you will likely see your company's performance flatline or decline.

Talented people with the desire to succeed is one of the key elements required to scale your business. Talented people like to work with other talented people, so build out your team accordingly.

STEP UP TO THE PLATE
Turning Ideas into Action

It's my hope that this book will be used for decades to come as a tool to teach others about how to become more successful in work and in life. I've mentioned many people in this book (and more to come) who have worked for, or currently work for, PFSbrands. I hope that these people decide to stay on board and continue to contribute to our future success. The reality in a culture like ours is that we are encouraging everyone to work toward improvement in their personal and professional lives.

Someone recently asked me about our turnover rate at PFSbrands. I did not know the answer to this question. While we track this number, it is not a number that we publicize or obsessively watch. Why? Because in a continuously learning and continuously improving culture it's incumbent upon the leadership to ensure that people are constantly "stepping up." Those who obsessively grow at the same rate or faster than the company will be the individuals eligible for promotions within the organization. They may also be at risk of leaving for greater opportunities than we can provide in the short term. While we'd prefer that they stay in some cases, we applaud them if they leave for a career advancement that makes a positive impact on their life. Those individuals who don't make an effort to continuously learn and improve will ultimately find themselves at another company. We train our leaders to not avoid the critical conversations with individuals who are not working toward improvement.

Topgrading and many of the unique hiring practices we have developed have enabled us to become better at finding those individuals who want to continuously learn. We've found that lifelong learners are a great fit at PFSbrands, so we've developed systems and processes that help us to recruit these types of individuals.

Questions to consider:

1. Are you keenly aware of your key strengths and weaknesses?

2. If you are an employee, are you doing your part to continuously improve? Are you a solid team player who others like to work with? What are you doing to strengthen key relationships at work and at home?

3. If you are an owner, president, or CEO do you have a leadership team? If so, do you have expectations in writing and are you holding your leaders accountable?

4. If you are a leader in a company, what key positions do you need to fill?

5. Is your HR department only focused on administrative duties, or does that group focus on team development too?

6. Have you considered the benefits of requiring job candidates to fill out a career history form? Why is a career history form more effective than a resume?

7. If you are tasked with leading others, do you routinely assess your team? You should routinely ask yourself: "knowing what I know now, could I hire this person today?"

8. If you are a leader, who needs to be coached up or coached out? Are you having the tough conversations and are you making the tough decisions?

CHAPTER 9

Mirror Gazing: How Assessments and Surveys Keep Your Team on Top

---

See, when you drive home today, you've got a big windshield on the front of your car. And you've got a little bitty rearview mirror. And the reason the windshield is so large and the rearview mirror is so small is because what's happened in your past is not near as important as what's in your future.

JOEL OSTEEN

Everybody's mind works a little bit differently. My mind definitely works in a forward-looking manner. My sister recently bought me some personalized pens that say: "Keep Looking Forward, Shawn Burcham." I've never been much of a history buff and I really have difficulty looking back in time. That's probably why I don't typically get too excited about class reunions, homecomings, etc.

With that being said, continuous improvement requires you to look to the past so you can make adjustments as you move forward. Just like you do within moments of rousing yourself out of bed in the morning, not long after my "awakening" from reading several business books, I decided it was time to look in the mirror.

Self-reflection is definitely not an easy thing to do. However, opening yourself up to criticism from others is especially difficult. But to grow and learn, to improve, it's the only sure way to make certain you're Keeping Score internally. Watching the game reel the day after a loss, or a win for that matter, while having the coaches and players critiquing everyone's performance is a critical part of competing to win.

> For PFSbrands to compete, I knew it would be necessary for those in leadership roles to do some self-reflection, to gain insight into their performance through assessments and surveys.

For PFSbrands to compete, I knew it would be necessary for those in leadership roles to do some self-reflection, to gain insight into their performance through assessments and surveys. And I also knew it wouldn't be an easy policy to adopt, so to set the expectation for others to follow, I went first.

I kept our first company-wide survey fairly simple, disseminating it electronically through Survey Monkey because anonymity was more likely to ensure good, solid feedback. The focus was open-ended questions. What are my greatest strengths? What are my greatest weaknesses? I also asked one of my favorite questions that I picked up from reading *Scaling Up*, by Verne Harnish: What do I need to start doing? What do I need to stop doing? What do I need to keep doing? This has evolved into one of my favorite questions to ask employees, customers, and suppliers. Here's a little more explanation:

Start

What is a habit you could start that can help you achieve your goals?

Stop

What are you doing today to prevent you from reaching your goals?

Keep

What can you do more of that is pushing you toward your goals?

The results didn't necessarily surprise me, but they confirmed some areas I needed to improve: be more patient, communicate more often, and share "why" we are doing things, share the company vision, keep the open-door policy and be more approachable, and delegate more. At that time in 2011 we had thirty-five or so employees, and I was in a headspace where, because I was able to be in contact with each person, I thought it was enough to ask someone to do something and just expect it to be done. No questions asked, no more needed to be said.

I wouldn't qualify my leadership style as authoritative; I just wasn't looking for feedback. And I probably thought I had more answers than I really did. I didn't capture the wisdom of my team. But I wasn't necessarily doing it on purpose. I think it was more of a time issue. I felt like I was efficient if I gave orders and moved on. That's one thing that I've really worked on over the last several years, making sure we had the "why" in place. We had a mission and a vision, but that was about it—not even a solid corporate strategy in writing. I just kept it all in my head and somehow expected others to "get it."

I was expecting our team to win, but hadn't clearly communicated the rules of the game for them. And if I wasn't doing a good enough job with thirty-five employees, it wasn't going to get any easier as we grew toward fifty or one hundred. That's about the time we developed our first senior leadership team. Ultimately, I enlisted their help with creating and fine-tuning the mission, the vision, our guiding principles, and our core values. We also began crafting annual strategic planning and working toward better budgeting processes.

Now, surveys have become a regular part of life at PFSbrands. We have team surveys for each department staggered throughout the year. Every single employee has an anonymous 360-degree survey done on them once per year. Anyone that wants to offer feedback on them is able to do so. And every individual participates in a specialized survey at the six-month mark. This allows them to give feedback on the company, their leaders, challenges, and much more. This provides our leadership team with valuable feedback.

We have financial literacy surveys, and third-party surveys such as "A Great Place to Work." Then we do Start, Stop, Keep surveys every month, and a Straight talk Question survey where people can send in anonymous questions. I answer these questions in our monthly huddle in what we call the Straight talk Zone.

Survey results definitely can sting, especially when you're new to it. But I can honestly say they've helped me grow personally and professionally. These surveys have contributed to the overall success at PFSbrands.

But they aren't for everyone.

NOT FOR THE FAINT-HEARTED

We did one of our peer-to-peer surveys for our middle leadership team (what we call our senior leadership advisory group) while offsite in 2016. It was an anonymous survey everyone had to fill out online, and then we read the results live … about everybody, *to* everybody.

What's really great about that format is when there's a tremendous consensus, you know as a leader that your people know each other well. For example with me, "patience" came up probably 80 percent of the time with 80 percent of the people. I would agree with that, and it shows that my team knows me. But for people who have not been through that kind of introspective process, that kind of consensus may not simply be eye opening, but overwhelming. By the way, I'm still not a patient person and I likely never will be. I have improved in this area, though. I'm also far more aware of it and I vocally make sure others are aware of it. Like most weaknesses, it is also a strength. I tell people that we'd never be in the great position that we are today if it wasn't for the fact that I'm not a patient person. This isn't necessarily uncommon for highly driven people, especially founders who scale companies.

In a round of surveys back in 2012, one employee in particular had no idea they were perceived by teammates as being somewhat controlling and moody. That's one of those defining moments where the feedback may feel hurtful or negative, but can be used to refine behavior and attitude. I've seen some significant changes in people as a result of these kinds of surveys, because folks don't always realize how they are being perceived. It provides an opportunity for a conversation, to sit down and effectively work through any issues.

> I've seen some significant changes in people as a result of these kinds of surveys, because folks don't always realize how they are being perceived.

To this day, my surveys reveal that I'm often perceived as someone who is intimidating to talk to. I perceive this feedback to come from individuals who are new or may not exude a large amount of self-confidence. However, it is certainly not how I like to be viewed (except by those boys dating my daughters). Being perceived as intimidating definitely has to do with my personality, my intense work ethic and drive. It also has to do with an extreme workload and desire to always be growing. But I've deliberately and sincerely tried to make adjustments, and when people get to know me, they see that I just have a very direct approach to getting to the root of a problem, as opposed to sitting and shooting the breeze for thirty minutes. As a pilot, I don't like circling the runway. It only wastes fuel and time.

That individual who was perceived as moody and controlling just wasn't able to take the criticism in stride and we eventually had to part ways. The attitude and behavior did improve quite a bit, but it never got to the point where it needed to be. Ultimately, you're making your company stronger by knowing where you stand with everybody, and by having them be able to look in the mirror.

One of the best tools for mirror gazing is the Kolbe Assessment.

WHAT IS THE KOLBE ASSESSMENT?

Kathy Kolbe was the first person to identify four universal human instincts used in creative problem-solving. These instincts are not measurable. However, the observable acts derived from them can be identified and quantified by the Kolbe A Index, and describe an individual's conative abilities.[14]

For a psychology refresher, there are essentially three parts that make up the human mind: how we think (cognitive), how we feel (affective), and how we go about taking action (conative).

---

14   Kolbe Corp., accessed June 4, 2019, http://kolbe.com.

Three Parts of the Mind

1. **COGNITIVE**	2. **CONATIVE**	3. **AFFECTIVE**
Thinking	*Doing*	*Feeling*
• IQ	• Drive	• Desires
• Skills	• Necessity	• Motivation
• Reason	• Innate force	• Attitudes
• Knowledge	• Instinct	• Preferences
• Experience	• Mental energy	• Emotions
• Education	• Talents	• Values

More than a million people hailing from all different cultures and backgrounds have completed the assessment, and it is currently used as a tool in some of the most successful companies in the world, from NASA to Oracle to American Express to Microsoft. The results provide a graphical representation of an individual's instinctive modus operandi (M.O.). There's no right or wrong result. The assessment simply provides insight into an individual's instinct-driven behaviors, represented in the four Kolbe Action Modes:

1. **FACT FINDER:** The instinctive way we gather and share information

2. **FOLLOW THRU:** The instinctive way we organize

3. **QUICK START:** The instinctive way we deal with risk and uncertainty

4. **IMPLEMENTOR:** The instinctive way we handle space and tangibles

Each of us has a unique combination of these behaviors, but the Kolbe Assessment allows us to determine exactly where on the scale we fall in each category. Most individuals have at least one Action

Mode that they initiate in, with the others placing somewhere on the scale in lesser degrees. And while you must always be cautious not to categorize someone based on their score, much can be inferred about the person based on their natural conative strengths.

Let's dig a little deeper into each Action Mode.

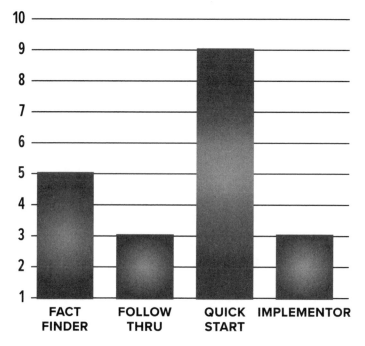

Shawn Burcham's results on the Kolbe A Index.

THE FACT FINDER

Fact Finder Initiating Actions: Strategize

People who Initiate Fact Finder Actions have the essential ability to specify, strategize, and define opportunities. When free to be themselves they gather information through their drive to:

- **DELIBERATE**
- **DIFFERENTIATE**
- **DOCUMENT**
- **DESIGNATE**

Having this zone of Fact Finder makes a person exceptionally thorough in weighing pros and cons and in evaluating opportunities. It means he or she can provide significant ingredients of problem-solving to assess probabilities and calculate odds. When striving toward a goal, this pragmatic approach determines realistic objectives.

THE FOLLOW THRU

Follow Thru Initiating Actions: Systematize

When using their instinctive strengths, people who Initiate Follow Thru Actions have a wonderful ability to provide the world with structured systems. Their natural drive is to consistently organize information and material, and put feelings and thoughts into context, which they do when they:

- **SEQUENCE**
- **CLASSIFY**
- **INTEGRATE**
- **COORDINATE**

This zone of Follow Thru Action is tied to a knack for bringing order out of chaos. People with this instinctive strength set trends, offer templates, and provide the boundaries within which we all work, play, and do just about everything in life. They carry out complicated tactics by sorting options, finding what's missing, and arranging a structured approach with both a Plan A and Plan B.

THE QUICK START
Quick Start Initiating Actions: Innovate

This one is me. My Kolbe score is a 5-3-9-3 with the 9 being in the Quick Start category and the 5 being in the Fact Finder category. When people who Initiate Quick Start Actions are in the zone, they innovate. Free them up to be themselves and they will open doors— and minds—by tackling uncertainty. They take risks and make deals when they have open-ended opportunities to:

- **IMPROVISE**
- **ORIGINATE**
- **PROMOTE**
- **ACCELERATE**

A person who naturally strives in this zone of Quick Start Action is authentic when taking on challenges—usually with a sense of urgency. They lead the way to visionary possibilities, creating what others said couldn't be done. Their best works happen when they are challenged to meet tough deadlines, play hunches, and switch from one option to another. Encourage them to speak up and they will learn what they are thinking as they hear themselves say it. Never underestimate the speed with which they can make things happen.

THE IMPLEMENTOR

Implementor Initiating Actions: Protect

It takes people who Initiate Implementor Actions to use the haptic sense of touch to literally make what it takes to get the world to go round. They provide an array of necessary and useful strengths, as they use the instinct that deals with space and tangibles to:

- **MANEUVER**
- **MANIPULATE**
- **MANUFACTURE**
- **MECHANIZE**

Initiating Implementor Actions involve an uncanny sense of where objects need to go and how to get them there. Haptics protect, construct, transport, and demonstrate the tangible goods of life. Their natural ability to build, to produce quality and substantial tangible solutions includes creating the machines and technology that make those things possible.[15]

KEEPING SCORE WITH KOLBE

I was first introduced to Kolbe by my good friend Mark Gandy, the same guy who converted me to a reader after PFSbrands had seen tremendous growth but was struggling to take additional cash to the bottom line. At the time he worked for B2B CFO, though today he administers assessments for companies and individuals through his firms G3CFO and Free Agent CFO. Mark is actually a Kolbe-certified consultant, having committed to some pretty intense training initially and continuing education every year. Since 2015, he's given nearly two hundred assessments.

---

15   Kathy Kolbe, *Striving Zones* (City: Publisher, 1985-2015). Used with permission.

At PFSbrands, the Kolbe A Index is primarily given to people who hold salaried positions, as we've found it a valuable tool to assess professionals, particularly those in very autonomous roles or leadership positions, with three main goals. The first of the goals of the Kolbe Assessment is to gain insight into the individual for the rest of the team. When a team is functioning at as high of a level as we are at PFSbrands, knowing exactly *how* to communicate with each other is critical. For instance, my team knows me all too well. Most aren't going to present me with a long, detailed report, knowing I work better with quick bullet points. I'll ask follow-up questions if I need to, but I like my information delivered as succinctly as possible.

The second goal is to gain insight into the individual's M.O. so we know what the best fit may be for them within a department, basically plug them into the right lane. Or as Jim Collins likes to say, get them in the right seat on the bus.

For example, there is sales … and then there's sales management—instinctively two very different mind-sets and M.O.s. The person in charge of a sales department better score high in the Follow Thru category, because remember those are people who are process driven and meticulous when it comes to order. A VP of sales on the other hand might have a Quick Start M.O.—not a lot of detail, going with their gut, more focused on the results than the process. That's why it's common for a lot of salespeople to fail or stress out when they are promoted to a role where they are required to lead other people. A great salesperson will rarely make a great sales leader.

When you are leading a fast-growing company, sometimes the demands of a role changes and someone with a different M.O. is needed. There will be times when a particular person aligns greatly with your core values but no longer has the correct skill set to perform well in their current role. It's important to recognize this and work to shift individuals into positions where they can excel. For example, in a fast-paced company with so many different brands rolling and things moving at lightning speed, a Fact Finder mentality in a critical position where decisions need to be made quickly can impede progress.

The third goal of the Kolbe Assessment is as a tool to provide insight during the hiring process and when strategically assembling a team.

BACK TO THE ABCs

Just like you can't play a game, let alone win, with all forwards in basketball, or all catchers in baseball, no company can succeed with all Quick Starts or all Fact Finders. In fact, that is part of the reason some businesses stall out, because they may have a board of directors or a senior leadership team made up of conative clones. The best leaders are those who surround themselves with individuals who have different skill sets.

You absolutely want to have a mix of individuals, because each Action Mode of the Kolbe Assessment has its own strengths and limitations, based on the conative demands of the

> The best leaders are those who surround themselves with individuals who have different skill sets.

underlying position. That's why it's imperative to use Kolbe to your advantage when hiring for a specific role or building a particular team for a particular purpose.

While the Kolbe A Index is designed for individuals, there are the Kolbe B and Kolbe C Indexes as well. The latter is designed specifically to identify the instinctual attributes and skill sets needed for a certain role in the eyes of the supervisor or manager.

For example, say you run a nonprofit and you have six board seats with one left to fill. You might want to employ a Kolbe C Index to discover what is needed. Perhaps you are looking for someone who can vet grants or private donations, which generally is a fact-finding instinct. Or you might be looking for some who can create a great vision and take decisive action, necessitating the skill set of a Quick Start.

We've had Mark do a Kolbe C in three or four different instances now. We've needed a specific kind of person for a role, such as VP of business development. Mark has our hiring manager fill out a Kolbe C Index so we can drill down into the attributes we should be looking for in a prospective hire. Then we match that to the applicant's Kolbe A Index score, having a measure to go by.

A word of warning: the Kolbe Assessment is not the be-all and end-all. In a corporate setting, it is one of *many* tools to be used in determining how well an individual fits a particular role in a particular team, and provides insight on how that person functions best. It's a great tool for making sure you're getting the right person for the right seat, especially if you've narrowed the field down to a couple of candidates.

And from a legal standpoint, at the time of this writing and to the best of my understanding, the Kolbe Assessment is one of the few tests that can be used to discriminate when hiring.

THE MIRROR IS A POWERFUL TOOL

Surveys and assessments are not silver bullets that will turn someone from their unproductive ways to the next employee of the month. They will not correct workplace dysfunction. Only solid coaching and a strong culture of Keeping Score can do that. What surveys and assessments are intended to do is raise to the surface the strengths and weaknesses within a company. To shine a light on the good, bad, and ugly.

Once things are out in the open, there's an opportunity to sit down with people and have some honest conversations about how to move forward as a better person and team member, ultimately allowing PFSbrands to live up to our core purpose: to help others become more successful in work and in life. It's a chance to help others reflect on their strengths and weaknesses and help them realize that everybody has them.

If you're going to do these types of peer-to-peer, individual surveys on people, however, you absolutely must be committed to using the information for the best interest of the person. And you also have to realize that, depending on your culture and company dynamic, changes to varying degrees will occur. Gaining better employee engagement and communication sometimes means you're going to lose people. And you should. How many sports teams do you see that have the exact same people year after year?

You must be comfortable with the fact that not everyone is going to make it through the process. But as a leader, it's your job to make sure that all changes happen in a responsible way. You need to get the right people in the right seats, and offboard when necessary. And as you grow, it's like going from coaching high school football to college football—you have to start doing things differently, because your competition is completely different. Then when you hit the pro level, it's a whole new world in terms of what you have to do as a player or a coach or a team.

> Gaining better employee engagement and communication sometimes means you're going to lose people. And you should.

Because it can be such a sensitive topic, I actually share my surveys without filtering anything. When the results come in, I just put them out there raw. I believe as a leader you have to be that open and willing to share those things with the people you're working with. They definitely get to know you a lot better, and they respect you for your transparency, not to mention you send a message and set the example that all isn't necessarily pretty, and no one is perfect, but we are all expected to hold ourselves accountable. Most of the time I can honestly say that I've received follow-up calls from people who thanked me for having those tough conversations with them, and said they're in a better place personally and professionally because of what they learned about themselves.

At PFSbrands, we do all kinds of surveys. They can be anonymous or not. Twice a year we do a simple net promoter score (NPS) survey internally that is anonymous. The survey questions are: (1) How likely (on a scale of zero to ten) are you to recommend PFSbrands as an employer to your friends or family members? (2) Why?

This is a great survey because it takes less than sixty seconds in most cases, we can benchmark our scores, and we get open feedback. It also creates some coaching opportunities and an avenue for me to provide company-wide communication on certain topics. Many leaders may want to avoid the difficult topics, but here's an example of how I replied to some recent feedback. The response came back with a five (on that zero to ten scale) and the comments were as follows:

> *This is a great place to work, but no advancement opportunities or increase in salaries. ESOP seems like a pipe dream. The SLT likes the status quo of keeping everyone in their place. Too many good employee-owners have left because there are better opportunities outside of here and our company does nothing to retain them. I wonder about my future long term with so many*

good workers leaving if we can sustain ourselves moving forward. Open-Book Management is a double-edged sword; we see a lot of money being spent with little question as to why it is being spent. I don't feel as an employee-owner I have a vote or say on my future, because SLT makes all the decisions and I think it should be left up to a company-wide vote. Also, reading books doesn't pay the bills or get the job done. There are a lot of other ways to learn that need to be looked at. I know a lot of people that are "book worms" but can't even "tie their shoe" or hold a regular job. I respect my job and give 110 percent when I am here, but these are my candid thoughts that bother me or think about if I were to recommend this company to someone else.

Here's the company-wide email I sent out:

First of all, thank you very much for the straight talk feedback. I can't say enough about how great it is when people express their true feelings. With that being said, I'd like to address your points one by one.

I'm glad you think PFSbrands is a great place to work. That gives me the desire to help you to become more successful in work & in life. Over the past twenty years we have advanced numerous people both professionally and financially. While we don't believe in annual pay raises, I can assure you that our leadership team is dedicated to providing increases to those that are aligned with our core values and producing consistent results. If you've gone consistently without increases and you are not aware of the reasoning, I'd encourage you to talk to your leader or come to me directly.

As for the ESOP being a pipe dream, I'd say that a 488 percent increase in the first year of our ESOP is phenomenal and unheard of. I'd encourage you to reach out to a leadership team member so we can share the long-term benefits of the ESOP. It is a complicated business model but I'm excited to see the financial benefits it provides employee-owners over the next ten to twenty years.

The senior leadership team is certainly not content with the status quo of keeping everyone in their place. In fact, just last week we elevated four individuals into various leadership positions.

Good employees will come and go. There's an old saying about a CFO asking a CEO: "What if we train our employees and they leave?" The CEO responds, "What if we don't and they stay?" We work extremely hard to help people become more successful in work and in life. I'm confident everyone that leaves here leaves with a better understanding of business than when they arrived. There are going to be times when the company outgrows certain people and times when people outgrow the company. Further, there is almost always "more to the story" than most employee-owners can be aware of. In fact, oftentimes through the resignation or termination process, along with the exit interview process, we actually find out more reasons why they were not a fit for PFSbrands. We are constantly talking to each individual employee-owner to evaluate whether there are cultural or performance concerns. Our goal is to always provide employee-owners who are not comfortable here an opportunity to make that decision on their own. If they can't make it on their own, we will make it for them. In the past twenty years I can honestly say that there are only two or three individuals that have exited that I would consider hiring back.

I wonder about your future here also. If you don't reach out to the leaders at PFSbrands and seek help, you will likely be one of those resigning or being terminated. Since you think it's a great place to work, I'd encourage you to maybe "look in the mirror" and determine if the problem may be on your end. Given the fact that 94 percent of the people working here think it's a great place to work, and given the fact that I know the leadership team wants to help people become more successful, why not reach out for help?

You have to spend money to make money. We're so open compared to virtually every other company in the world. If you want to know why we are spending money on something, there are so many avenues for you to ask those questions. You can ask any leader directly, you can ask in an anonymous survey, you can ask in a huddle, or you can even shoot me an email and ask.

Successful companies don't become successful by allowing everyone to "vote." However, at PFSbrands we provide numerous opportunities for EVERY employee-owner to provide feedback. In fact, every quarter we provide a company-wide survey to solicit feedback on what each person feels is most important for the next quarter. Successful companies need good leaders. Those leaders are tasked with making some decisions on their own and soliciting feedback and allowing groups to make decisions when it makes sense.

As for reading books, we don't require anyone (other than the senior leadership team and the senior leadership advisory group) to read if they don't want to. However, to be a good employee-owner you need to be able to see the vision and understand why we do some of the things we do. In order to do that, you need to read some relevant books. Ultimately, you'll probably never make it to a leadership position at PFSbrands if you don't read or listen to books. Not just because of the sole fact that you didn't read, but because you didn't capture the knowledge necessary to be on the same level as the rest of the leadership team.

On a final note, I personally don't know anyone that can't "tie their shoe." If you wouldn't mind, lend them a hand and teach them. That would help them to become more successful in work & in life. Maybe even buy them a book on how to tie their shoe. They might enjoy reading it since they are a book worm.

PFSbrands is not right for everyone. That's why we work so hard in the interview process to determine who to hire. I'm here to help if you're willing to accept some coaching.

As you can see, I like to address issues with a straight talk approach. The truth is, a leader is never going to be liked by *everyone*. You're never going to make everybody happy doing the right thing for the company, or for the team overall. Keeping Score means that sometimes you have to make hard decisions, such as implementing a policy of mirror gazing. And those hard decisions should be explained, though not everybody is going to be happy.

But if you handle it properly, you will be respected.

Glance back occasionally, but keep looking forward most of the time!

STEP UP TO THE PLATE
Turning Ideas into Action

Regardless of whether you are a leader or an employee, you should be well aware of your mode of operations. How do you think and how do you process information? Further, you should know your strengths and weaknesses better than anyone else. You should SEEK OUT THIS INFORMATION through the many tools available.

If you are a leader, then you need to become acutely aware of these qualities in other individuals. If you make a living selling, you should become acutely aware of how others process information. It's imperative when working with other people is a critical part of your life that you understand how they function.

If you are a company leader, make sure you begin utilizing surveys to improve your business. If you are an owner, president, or CEO start with a company-wide survey on yourself in a first step to build greater trust in your organization. If you need help implementing surveys, there will be some contact information in the bonus chapter.

Questions and items to consider:

1.   What are your greatest strengths?

2.   What are your greatest weaknesses?

3.   What do you need to start, stop, and keep doing to better yourself?

4.   Take the Kolbe Assessment so you know your M.O.

5.   If you are a leader, do an anonymous survey on yourself and allow everyone in your organization to participate. Share the results with everyone.

6. If you are a leader, do a Kolbe Assessment on your key managers so you know their M.O. Sit down and talk about it. Adjust your leadership style when you are communicating with each individual. Based on your limited knowledge on Kolbe, can you think of any person who you want to keep who happens to be in the wrong role?

CHAPTER 10

ESOP's Fables: The Fact and Fiction behind Embracing an Employee Stock Ownership Plan

If everyone is moving forward together,
then success takes care of itself.
HENRY FORD

When I think back to 2011, to when PFSbrands was going through that challenging time of spinning our wheels and not getting the traction we needed to reach our potential, of all the questions running through my head, the real question I remember asking was: "What am I doing here on the planet?"

As I've mentioned, I've always had tremendous respect and admiration for the kind of life-changing work my father dedicated his career to. I also knew it takes a special person to do that kind of work. But one day I realized that maybe we weren't so different in our career goals after all—trying to help others, setting them up for success. I love creating jobs. I love creating opportunities for people and sharing in the excitement of those who actually grab that opportunity and do something with it. Even though I had subconsciously done it my entire life, I didn't really have that purpose at the front of my mind until 2011, when I really figured out that's what I like to do, that's what I'm good at, and that's what I'm really passionate about.

And that's when I knew becoming an ESOP company was part of the future of PFSbrands.

SO WHAT'S AN ESOP?

An employee stock ownership plan (ESOP) is an employee benefit plan similar in many ways to a profit-sharing plan. Simply put, it's a qualified retirement plan similar to a 401(k). It essentially turns employees into employee-*owners* by providing them an opportunity to benefit in the overall value of the company they work for. Employees are issued shares of stock over time, without paying anything for these shares.

A 2000 Rutgers study found that ESOP companies grow 2.3 percent to 2.4 percent faster after setting up their ESOP than would have been expected without it. And companies that combine employee-ownership with employee workplace participation programs, such as OBM, show even more substantial gains in performance.[16] A 1986 National Center for Employee Ownership (NCEO) study found that employee-ownership firms that practice participative management grow 8 percent to 11 percent per year faster with their ownership

---

16   "Research on Employee Ownership, Corporate Performance, and Employee Compensation," National Center for Employee Ownership, accessed April 9, 2019, https://www.nceo.org/articles/research-employee-ownership-corporate-performance.

plans than they would have without them.[17]

Not only do companies benefit, but so do the employee-owners. A 1997 Washington State study found that ESOP participants made 5 percent to 12 percent more in wages and had almost three times the retirement assets as did workers in comparable non-ESOP companies.[18]

ESOPs can be found in all kinds and sizes of companies. Some of the more notable companies that are majority owned by employees are Publix Super Markets (182,500 employees), Lifetouch (21,000 employees), W. L. Gore and Associates (maker of Gore-Tex, 10,000 employees), and Davey Tree Expert (8,260 employees). In fact, companies with ESOPs and other broad-based employee-ownership plans account for well over half of *Fortune*'s "100 Best Companies to Work for in America" list year after year.

THE JOURNEY TOWARD ESOP

Our journey to becoming a 100 percent employee-owned company really began in the late 2000s as we were starting to grow. I was familiar with the ESOP model because of my experience with supermarkets. That particular industry happens to be a great candidate for an ESOP because of the low profit margins associated with supermarkets. These low margins, along with the complicated tax laws associated with selling a business, make an ownership transition very difficult when an owner is ready to retire. As I continued to research the concept, I was amazed at how other businesses had become successful by creating an ESOP. Outside of grocery stores, there are other hotbed industries that thrive as ESOPS, such as construction, engineering, architects,

---

17   Ibid.
18   Ibid.

and manufacturing.

The overall model had always been appealing to me because it gives everybody an opportunity to have some "sweat equity" in the company—providing the ultimate manifestation of ownership thinking. Employee-owners have something bigger to work for because they're earning shares of stock, and they have the ability to work for a company that can make that share price go up. Keeping Score takes on a new meaning with an ESOP. And from a financial standpoint, I knew there were substantial tax advantages for me as the selling shareholder and also for the new employee-owners.

> Employee-owners have something bigger to work for because they're earning shares of stock, and they have the ability to work for a company that can make that share price go up.

So investigating the ESOP model was one of Trevor Monnig's first orders of business when he was brought onboard as the CFO of PFSbrands. He actually came into the position with zero information about ESOPs. He and I worked hand in hand for the first year and a half to get up to speed on the ESOP landscape—traveling to conferences, networking, researching, and educating ourselves on every aspect of the model.

TOO GOOD TO BE TRUE?

What we found after all those months of investigation and research was that moving to an ESOP model would definitely be a complicated process. The shares in an ESOP are not exactly stocks in the traditional sense. We wouldn't give out stock certificates to employees of

PFSbrands like a publicly held company such as Apple might. Even in a privately held company, there would be a stock ledger to track activity and individual accounts.

Instead, the ESOP is a participatory way of providing ownership to the employee through a trust, with what is called *participatory stock*. Without getting too technical, all this means is that 100 percent of those shares are owned by the trust, and the employees as participants of the trust, through the eligibility requirements defined in the plan document, participate in that ownership of the trust. Within the plan, all shares flow through and are allocated to participant accounts.

But first you have to find agreeable terms with the buyer, as well as the seller. It's a true negotiation, an acquisition transaction. I would literally have to sell my company. And rightly so, it would require all the legal points, the attorneys, the valuators, and all the other professional services to push it across the finish line. As any founder will tell you, this is not an easy decision. Founders are tied to their businesses emotionally, and working through all of these emotions is incredibly difficult. This was especially tough in my case, since I was not near ready to retire or leave the business.

But the benefits to all involved, we found, were incredible.

It's the ultimate form of employee engagement. You're giving real ownership to the people who help to make the company successful. They, too, get to reap the rewards and the results of all that hard work. Not to mention it's a second retirement plan to build future wealth at PFSbrands, right alongside their 401(k). The profitability and cash flow performance of the company and their future wealth is directly impacted by their actions each day.

You can talk all day about thinking like an owner and trying to get people to act like it. When you tie in this reward that is extremely performance based, then all of a sudden you get that pull toward action and good decision-making for the long term.

Personally, I believe "it's the best capital model on the planet." From a financial perspective, an S-corporation that is 100 percent employee-owned by an ESOP doesn't pay federal or state income taxes. That frees up cash flow to purchase the stock from the selling shareholder, grow the business faster, and ultimately have cash to fund the required repurchase obligations as employee-owners leave or retire. So instead of sending nearly half of our profits to Uncle Sam each year, we use that capital to invest in our business and to create more jobs. The federal and state income taxes are ultimately paid by the stockholders whenever they cash out, which can only be done if they leave or retire. Individual workers are typically at a lower tax rate than what a company would be paying each year. Again, this is similar to how taxes are treated if employees invest in a 401(k) retirement plan.

The other main benefit of an ESOP is that it can be used to protect the jobs of employees and protect the community you live in. Unfortunately, many companies neglect to do any type of succession planning. Oftentimes, these companies just "die" and don't exist after the owner retires or passes away. Obviously when this happens, the jobs of any employees simply go away.

More and more business owners are deciding to sell their companies to private equity firms or larger companies within their industry. I've personally seen the postsale effect this has had on companies with great people and great cultures. Oftentimes, when private equity firms or larger companies purchase companies, they close down local factories and offices, thus leaving the local community or state without these jobs. In cases where employees do manage to keep their local jobs, most often the entire corporate culture is turned upside down and these employees are left with a much different working environment.

In either case, a lot of times the community that the business was a part of suffers. PFSbrands, for example, is a big part of a small community here. The city of Holts Summit has been good to us; we mean a lot to them. Selling out to a larger company could mean the company suddenly moves out of state making all those local jobs go away.

There's not one particular thing that triggers a company to go the ESOP route, but for us we knew it was a win-win-win situation. It's a win for me as the founder, a win for the employee-owners, and certainly a win for the community.

It's just a very evergreen way to run a business. I honestly don't know that there's a better win-win-win business model out there. Every politician and lobbyist within federal and state governments should be looking at the ESOP model and finding more ways to simplify it while encouraging business owners to consider this structure. Those who are truly interested in helping this country and helping others to become more successful should be embracing ESOPs. Unfortunately, you just don't hear enough about ESOPs. In fact, the concept is rarely taught in business schools across the country.

According to the NCEO,[19] ESOPs have a number of significant tax benefits, the most important of which are as follows:

1. *Contributions of stock are tax deductible:* That means companies can get a current cash flow advantage by issuing new shares or treasury shares to the ESOP, although this means existing owners will be diluted.

2. *Cash contributions are deductible:* A company can contribute cash on a discretionary basis year to year and take a tax deduction for it, whether the contribution is used to buy

---

19 "How an Employee Stock Ownership Plan (ESOP) Works," National Center for Employee-ownership (NCEO), accessed April 9, 2019, www.nceo.org/articles/esop-employee-stock-ownership-plan.

shares from current owners or to build up a cash reserve in the ESOP for future use.

3. *Contributions used to repay a loan the ESOP takes out to buy company shares are tax deductible:* The ESOP can borrow money to buy existing shares, new shares, or treasury shares. Regardless of the use, the contributions are deductible, meaning ESOP financing is done in pretax dollars.

4. *Sellers in a C corporation can get a tax deferral:* In C corporations, once the ESOP owns 30 percent of all the shares in the company, the seller can reinvest the proceeds of the sale in other securities and defer any tax on the gain.

5. *In S corporations, the percentage of ownership held by the ESOP is not subject to income tax at the federal level (and usually the state level as well):* That means, for instance, that there is no income tax on 30 percent of the profits of an S corporation with an ESOP holding 30 percent of the stock, and no income tax at all on the profits of an S corporation wholly owned by its ESOP. Note, however, that the ESOP still must get a pro rata share of any distributions the company makes to owners.

6. *Dividends are tax deductible:* Reasonable dividends used to repay an ESOP loan, passed through to employees, or reinvested by employees in company stock are tax deductible.

7. *Employees pay no tax on the contributions to the ESOP, only the distribution of their accounts, and then at potentially favorable rates:* The employees can roll over their distributions in an IRA or other retirement plan or pay current tax on the distribution, with any gains accumulated over time taxed as

capital gains. The income tax portion of the distributions, however, is subject to a 10 percent penalty if made before normal retirement age.[20]

THE NEGATIVES

We all know that everything has a catch. So what are some of the downsides of an ESOP?

The biggest hurdle for any business owner, especially if you decide to sell more than 50 percent of your company to an ESOP, is reconciling that somebody else owns the company. So instead of a two-person board of directors, which was Julie and me, we now have an official board of directors. So the owner has to be comfortable with the reality that you have to operate your company with more "formality."

> The biggest hurdle for any business owner, especially if you decide to sell more than 50 percent of your company to an ESOP, is reconciling that somebody else owns the company.

ESOPs can also be expensive to set up and investigate. Because the ESOP concept is so unique, there are many things to learn and explore as a business owner considers whether or not an ESOP is right for them. Both time and money can be a deterrent for owners who are already busy.

There's definitely more structure that has to be put in place, more paperwork, more red tape, more of what I would call "bureaucracy." These are things that entrepreneurs and founders aren't exactly fond of. Many owners are used to calling all the shots, doing exactly what they want, not really answering to anybody, not documenting anything if

20 Ibid.

they don't want to. All that has to change if you're going to implement an ESOP correctly.

Because of the bureaucracy and costs, a company has to be a certain size to establish an ESOP. Because of the complexity and red tape involved, small companies and start-up companies usually can't afford the ESOP structure. This is unfortunate, especially in today's world, where you have so many people that want to "give back" to others. If our government made it easier and removed a lot of the costs associated with the ESOP structure, I'm confident that we would see more small companies establishing partial or 100 percent employee-owned companies. Further, if our schools and universities began to educate our youth and young adults on ESOPs, we would undoubtedly see more of them. It would be awesome to be able to set up an ESOP with about as much effort as it takes to set up an LLC, S corporation, or C corporation.

Another turnoff for some business owners, specifically those who wish to maximize how much they put in their pockets, is that the ESOP has to be a fair market value. You can't create an ESOP model and get the type of return on investment that you could get if somebody was to come in from a private equity firm, or a bigger company coming in for a strategic buyout. As a seller establishing an ESOP, you oftentimes leave money on the table to do what you feel is the right thing: to give everybody that stake in the outcome.

That being said, PFSbrands doesn't operate much differently now that we are an ESOP. On January 3, 2017, we made the transaction. On January 4, it was operating the same way. I can remember the first Saturday after the sale, my oldest daughter, Claudia, asked my wife where I was.

Julie said, "He's at the office."

"Oh, so really nothing's changed," Claudia replied.

THE RIGHT TEAM

This can't be overstated enough: any owner looking to move toward an ESOP model must have two key people completely on board and in place—the CFO and HR director.

I had actually talked about ESOPs throughout the interview process with Trevor, well before we even brought him on as our CFO. It was a model that I was very intrigued with and really wanted to investigate, but I needed some help. Strategically, that was a factor in hiring him, to help PFSbrands navigate the research and the transaction. As for HR, what we now call People Success, thankfully we already had Carla, who got more involved down the road as we were making the final decisions to go the ESOP route. And she was even more instrumental and involved *after* the transaction because of the effect on Human Resources.

The person leading your HR department must be supportive of the ESOP and they must be willing to take on a whole new level of communication. There are more administrative functions involved to track each person's stock in the ESOP, annual audits have to take place, and annual stock certificates need to be compiled for each employee-owner.

FIVE TRAITS OF AN EFFECTIVE ESOP LEADER

ESOP companies are special and unique. When done correctly, employee-ownership creates a culture of employees who are actively involved in the business on all levels. Employee-owners can and do participate fully in every aspect of company management and growth. Engagement in this type of company is unrivaled and helps ESOPs outperform other types of companies. Because of this, ESOPs require a distinct type of leader, with distinct characteristics.

Low Ego, High Self-Esteem

A healthy ESOP leader is willing to admit mistakes and is not afraid to admit to failure. Most importantly, they learn from mistakes and failure. An effective ESOP leader has no need for an ego, but has high self-esteem. A confident, competent leader will be best and this type of leadership will foster and encourage the best aspects of ESOP culture.

Master Communicator

A great public speaker has a huge advantage—but it's not just about giving speeches, it's about communicating with employee-owners. Employee-owners want to understand how things are going with their company (their ESOP), and they deserve to know. An executive who can communicate openly in many forms will lead the team the most effectively. Communicating the vision of the company frequently is most beneficial.

Visionary

In a successful ESOP, turnover is low and typical long-term employees tend to be more averse to change. It's important that leaders continue to emphasize with all employee-owners that growth involves taking risks and there will be failures along the way. It is important for ESOPs to keep evolving and growing. It's vital to have a leader who can enforce a vision of growth and innovation. ESOPs must continue to evolve and change to meet market demands like any other company.

Faithful Listener

Feedback is crucial in soliciting employee-owners' thoughts and ideas. The best leaders of ESOPs are active and authentic when listening to their peers. Not all ideas can be implemented; however, they can be heard. Great leaders know how to solicit feedback and actually enjoy doing it.

Action Taker

Making decisions and executing effectively is necessary for a successful ESOP leader. While an ESOP is made up of many employee-owners, leaders still need to be able and willing to make decisions, especially the tough ones. The top leaders will decide when they need to listen to all points of view, when they need to solicit limited feedback, and when they need to make decisions on their own. An ESOP does not provide every employee-owner an entitlement to be involved in every decision. Great leaders will make the best decisions possible for executing a plan.

Talented or not, the best ESOP leaders encase these five characteristics. Without these key attributes a leader is destined for failure in an ESOP environment. It takes a leader just as special and unique as the ESOP itself.

Everybody Wins

A lot of owners go to an ESOP model because they think it's the magic pill to create employee engagement and get a better culture. But if you don't teach employees about the business, about the rules of the game, about the importance of Keeping Score, then that culture will never evolve.

When Trevor and I were making the rounds during our investigation phase toward the ESOP model, we often found ourselves as the cultural and employee engagement experts within the groups. Not to say there weren't companies out there with positive and productive cultures, but there were so many leaders in these organizations looking for ways to improve their culture and improve their employee engagement, and even looking at how to implement Open-Book Management. In fact, Patrick Carpenter says that from all of his experience, only about 15 to 20 percent of these ESOP companies actually practice Open-Book Management.[21] Again I have to ask: How can a team play to win when they don't even know the rules of the game and they're not Keeping Score?

We found ourselves way ahead in that space—the employee engagement, the Open-Book Management, and the culture. The ESOP model for our employees was the icing on the cake.

At our PFSbrands headquarters, we now fly a flag outside the office, one that we put up during our twentieth anniversary celebration, demonstrating that we are extremely proud of being 100 percent employee-owned. And that's because I strongly believe that the ESOP transaction, and the work we did to get there, will impact the lives of our employee-owners and their families for many generations to come.

Shawn and Julie with the "Employee Owned" flag
that flies at the PFSbrands headquarters.

Becoming an employee-owner is not the same as becoming an employee. When you become an employee-owner, you accept a position that can really make a difference—not only for yourself, but

---

21   Patrick Carpenter, personal communication with author, June 15, 2018.

212

also for your peers, for the business, and for the community.

I'll be the first to admit that our ESOP at PFSbrands has helped us to attract some of the best workers in the country. Our team members are interested in being involved, they are interested in learning how business works, and they want to know how they can contribute to ongoing success. People who have these traits, and those individuals that fit our overall culture, thrive in our fast-paced environment.

A UNIQUE ENVIRONMENT

Our ESOP allows us to create an environment where our people can excel, regardless of seniority or pay rate. Each individual consistently discovers new ways that they can positively impact our results. This takes a level of commitment that is above average, and when everyone is working on this level, it's amazing what we can accomplish together.

It's also important to communicate to employee-owners what an ESOP is NOT. Here's a recommended list from the National Center for Employee-ownership that helps to better explain some of the misperceptions of ESOPs and some cautionary points:

- No right to see salaries
- No right to be involved in every project
- No right to vote on every decision
- There is still a leadership team
- It's everyone's job to be happy
- Make money and generate cash
- Our real business is education
- Don't be overly risk averse
- Be creative and innovative
- Don't let the ESOP become a distraction[22]

---

22 Shawn Burcham, email message, June 2, 2018.

HAVING A VOICE

Everyone has a voice at PFSbrands. As employee-owners, everyone contributes to the success of our company. As part of our communication strategy, we have developed an ESOP committee. This committee is tasked with overall ESOP education and communication. We welcome ideas and comments—how we can make things better, more efficient, and more profitable. When tasked with responsibility, employee-owners consistently find ways to improve in their areas.

I have never believed in motivating people. I have always felt that the real key is to hire motivated people and then put them in an environment where they can excel. Engaged employee-owners are fun to work with and they will go the extra mile for their customers as well as their peers.

STEP UP TO THE PLATE
Turning Ideas into Action

As you can probably tell, I'm passionate about ESOPs. However, I realize that they are not right for everyone. Further, for owners who are considering a sale, timing is everything. As founders, Julie and I put a lot of money, time, and "sweat equity" into building PFSbrands. Like any other founder or owner, we expected some type of return on our investment. We elected the ESOP route so that we could truly make an impact on the future lives of our employee-owners and their families. In reality, we've just provided the *opportunity* for our current and future employee-owners. It's going to be fun to see them excel.

Very few companies provide the benefit of an ESOP and PFSbrands is proud to be 100 percent employee-owned. It's not just a job ... it's a future.

Items to consider:

1. ESOPs are very unique and not right for everyone. Do your personality and leadership style match the five traits of an effective ESOP leader?

2. If you are interested in learning more about ESOP visit www.nceo.org and www.esopassociation.org.

3. If you want to learn more about ESOPs and possibly getting help with a transition visit www.grittbusiness-coaching.com.

4. What fears or concerns do you have about ESOPs? Would an ESOP work for your company? Why or why not?

CHAPTER 11

Scaling for Success: How to Continually Up Your Company's Game

---

It takes a helluva long time to create an overnight success.

SHAWN BURCHAM

I n 2008, I was in a position where I could pretty much call up my banker and get more funds for whatever PFSbrands needed—inventory, accounts receivable growth, adding personnel in order to allow us to scale. We were growing fast. We went from $13 million to $24 million in sales within just a couple years. This was happening as one of the worst recessions of all time hit the United States.

Like a lot of banks, ours got caught up with a few bad loans and eventually got locked down by the federal government. They weren't allowed to loan money anymore, and ultimately ended up getting sold to another bank. All of a sudden, I didn't have access to growth capital by picking up the phone.

Mind you, this was before I'd met Mark Gandy, so I was still doing the accounting work and "managing the numbers" mostly by myself. That was a challenging time for us. A lot of things hit at once. With a growth rate that large comes people challenges. We were onboarding folks without much of a process, trying to manage the personnel by basically throwing people into the job and expecting them to "get it." We had a few people, some of them still with us today, who could pick it up on the fly. Others just didn't make it.

We've never been a super-capital-intensive type of company, but at that time we were really tight on freezer space. Trucks needed to be bought as we were growing, so new drivers were coming on all the time. Over-the-road truck drivers were fairly new to us. These individuals require different recruiting techniques and completely different training. In addition to more trucks and drivers, we also needed more office space, warehouse space, more freezer space, more coolers, more trailers, more computers, more field personnel—all at the same time.

I knew I couldn't wait for the situation with my bank to improve. Being bought out would take time, much longer than I could wait for capital if we were going to keep growing. After some searching, I ultimately found another bank ... one that wasn't in financial trouble. That whole process actually improved our company quite a bit, as it was a larger bank that required more structure and a different way of looking at financials.

It was a little bit of an education for me, but at the end of the day, I got through that process and from 2009 to 2015 built a great relationship with that particular bank, continuing to scale at double-digit, top-line growth. And then, in 2017, we moved to an ESOP model and realized they just weren't a viable candidate to loan money for an ESOP transaction. They didn't focus in that space, so we had to move on.

There are so many complexities involved with growing a company. If you've been a parent and raised kids, you can relate it to the various ages of your kids. Much like your kids need different things at different ages, your business has different needs at different stages of growth. I was able to migrate through those challenges at PFSbrands by continuously learning and improving. I was open to coaching and always open to change. By reading and listening to some of the best business and leadership thought leaders in the world, I was able to create my own way of Keeping Score at PFSbrands.

Scaling is never easy, but over time you definitely gain more than you lose. It's easy to know when to add. The key is knowing when to let go. As Verne Harnish says: "Letting go and trusting others to do things well is one of the more challenging aspects of being a leader of a growing organization."[23]

LEARNING OR LEAVING

This speaks to the Topgrading process. In a company that scales, you have to constantly be evaluating your people. I mentioned this at the end of chapter 9, but imagine a growth line that's going up at a forty-five-degree angle, and the company is on a path of learning and growing at that trajectory, but your personal line of learning and growth is horizontal; at some point that company is going to outgrow you. If you're not learning, then you're not improving. However, if you commit to learning and continuous improvement, you can follow that line up and ride with that company as long as you want. I'll use Dave Yarbrough as an example here. Dave is currently our senior vice president of business development and field operations. Dave doesn't have a college education, but instead learned the ropes at a young

---

23 Verne Harnish, *Scaling Up: How a Few Companies Make It ... and Why the Rest Don't (Rockefeller Habits 2.0)* (Ashburn: Gazelles, Inc., 2014).

age after high school with Steak 'n Shake. Dave started as a territory manager (now called business advisor) here at PFSbrands and he's fully embraced our culture and the many changes that have occurred. He has committed to improving personally, while holding himself and his team accountable as he transitioned into leadership roles. His advancement into a critical leadership role, at a young age, is a testament to his servant leadership style and his desire to help others to become more successful.

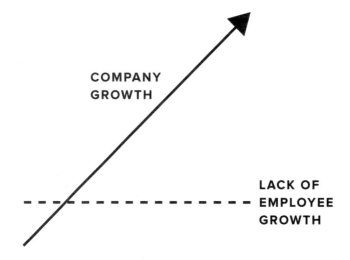

I see this desire to consistently improve at home as well. I've watched my middle daughter, Payton, dance since she was three years old: ballet, jazz, tap, and hip-hop. She's passionate about honing her skills, and at the age of eighteen she has recently been accepted to the University of Alabama to major in their dance program. She has an incredible work ethic and it's great to see her consistently improving her skills. I've consistently told her and my other two daughters that they can accomplish absolutely anything they want. To accomplish anything, first you have to BELIEVE.

Verne Harnish mentioned this quote in his book *Scaling Up*:

The #1 demotivator for talented people is having to put up with bozos, as Steve Jobs would call them. Nothing is more frustrating for "A" Players than having to work with "B" and "C" Players who slow them down and suck their energy. In that sense, "The best thing you can do for employees—a perk better than foosball or free sushi—is hire only "A" players to work alongside them. Excellent colleagues trump everything else.[24]

Scaling requires your team to evolve, but it also requires new blood. As a company is growing, sometimes there are simply some positions where you just have to go out and recruit the talent to help you get to that next level. I always want to promote from within if possible. But if we don't have the right fit for the position, then we go out and get them. Trevor is a great example of that. He fit the culture perfectly, and he brought experience from larger companies that we really needed. He also brought leadership that we really needed.

Another example of a time where we needed to look externally for a candidate is when we reached a level of complexity in our operations area. We needed a vice president of operations who had experience in warehousing, manufacturing, and logistics. Brock Blaise came on as that individual and now serves as our senior vice president of operations and leads logistics, the warehouse, print shop, manufacturing, marketing, and customer success. Brock came from Unilever, which was a billion-dollar company. While he was making more money at Unilever, Brock was ready for a life change, a change where he could bring his knowledge from a larger company to a smaller company that was better aligned with his personal values. Based on his current position and responsibility, I'm sure you can conclude that he's embraced our culture of continuous learning and improvement.

---

24   Ibid.

Oftentimes after I made key hires like these, I'd receive survey feedback like: "We're hiring too many chiefs and not enough Indians," or, "We need to be promoting from within." As a leader, you need to be able to weed through the negative comments and do what you know is best for the company and its future success. The individuals who provide comments like this don't know what they don't know.

> As a leader, you need to be able to weed through the negative comments and do what you know is best for the company and its future success.

In the end, we have a mix of home-grown leaders, and those who we've recruited to help us scale to the next level. And for those who were unwilling to engage in learning and Keeping Score, we had to part ways.

As counterintuitive as it may seem, occasionally we even have to part ways with some of our retail partners. Not all business is "good business."

PROTECTING THE BRAND

In 2014, we decided to take Champs Chicken to a franchise model. Prior to that we operated as a license model, which was a pretty simple two-page agreement. However, we started getting more and more products, really developing much better systems and processes, and really beginning to develop a great reputation for quality food. The overarching goal was to build the brand image and have even better control over the quality of food and service at the consumer level, one of the keys to scaling in food service.

We knew that caloric mandates and nutritional information guidelines were coming down from the FDA. That meant we were going to have to put that now -familiar caloric content on our menu boards. We knew it would be a three- to five-year process of selecting and migrating and coaching those retailers who we felt could ultimately do our brand justice, those we wanted to keep with our flagship Champs Chicken brand. The others, those who were just not aligned with the necessary commitment level, we moved to Cooper's Express or Private Label as an alternative path. We still valued these customers greatly; we just wanted to ensure that they were set up for success with the right program. Because of the federal franchise regulations, the FDA laws, and our desire to position the brand for greater success, we needed to have fully committed Champs Chicken operators.

Every company goes through those types of challenges as they work to elevate their business or their brand. I don't enjoy dictating to people what standards they need to follow. But at the end of the day, national franchise brands must have controls in place, or else they won't be able to build brand loyalty. If you go into McDonald's and you get a Big Mac or a Quarter Pounder, you want that Big Mac or Quarter Pounder to taste the same in every location. That's ultimately what every national brand is working toward, and it's what we're striving to do with Champs Chicken and BluTaco.

We still see some of our competitors that offer food-service brands in supermarkets and convenience stores with some really loose standards. I do think since the FDA has implemented recent nutritional and caloric laws, some of this is beginning to tighten up. However, a lot of our competitors in this space just don't work to mutually align goals with their customers. So, in some cases, we lose business to these competitors that are "lenient" and have lower standards, but I think we're much better at getting committed operators on board for our Champs Chicken and our BluTaco program today. Much like hiring the right people, we work hard to select the right customers.

EMBRACING THE FUTURE

Scaling is all about embracing the future. And in terms of workforce, millennials will make up 75 percent of the workforce by 2025.[25]

For the record, I'm not a big proponent of labels. I don't like putting people in a box and ultimately classifying millennials as lazy, or saying they don't have a work ethic. I don't believe this. I do think our country has a different work ethic today than it did in past generations. Some of this is a result of not having the blue-collar jobs like we used to. Kids just grow up in different environments than before. With that being said, I think there were problems in past generations and there are problems in current generations. However, if you know what you are looking for in employees, if you treat them with respect, then there are people out there who truly want to do a great job at work.

The biggest change I see is that the newer generations entering the workforce have to know the "why." They want to know why they're doing it, and that makes a lot of sense when you think about how they grew up with their devices. They have been able to get answers anytime they want them. I see it in my kids. If they want something, they want it now, and they want to know why … because that's the world they've known, thanks to technology.

> I believe that Open-Book Management cracks the code of millennials. It engages them. It gives them the information.

They are accustomed to instant gratification because of this technology they've grown up with.

The way we're running PFSbrands is the way of the future. Why?

---

25 Debra Donston-Miller, "Workforce 2020: What You Need to Know," *Forbes*, May 5, 2016, www.forbes.com/sites/workday/2016/05/05/workforce-2020-what-you-need-to-know-now/#54ad838d2d63.

Because millennials thrive in our Open-Book Management environment and I believe future generations will as well. I believe that Open-Book Management cracks the code of millennials. It engages them. It gives them the information.

In fact, Trevor gave a speech to the University of Missouri MBA students about Open-Book Management, specifically geared toward millennials. He said, "I highly recommend that when you come out with your MBA and you're looking for employment, you think about the culture and the environment that you're entering. You should be looking for an Open-Book Management company. And beyond that, an ESOP company."[26]

Imagine millennials going into a closed-book environment. They're going to work fifty hours a week on a need-to-know basis. How engaged do you think they're going to be? They might come in very engaged. They want to change the world. They want to do good things. I believe the environment at PFSbrands perpetuates that and allows them to do it and find satisfaction. However, if you put them in a need-to-know environment where they get information sparingly, or they start connecting the dots and find they don't add up, then they go from being an engaged employee to a disengaged employee in a very short time.

Millennials want truth and honesty. They value that. Transparency and Open-Book Management build trust. There's nothing hidden. Personal growth, education, and continuous learning are actually what this group is looking for. If companies today want to scale, then they need to embrace millennials and work to create an environment where they are engaged.

---

26 Trevor Moning, "Open-Book Management" (speech, University of Missouri, Columbia, Missouri, February 20, 2018).

TAKE YOUR TIME BACK AND GROW YOUR BUSINESS

What's your most valuable commodity? For me, the answer to that question is "my TIME." Each of us only has so much time … and when it's gone you can never get it back. That's why I fly airplanes!

Any leader who wants to scale should place a certain value on their time in order to be efficient in business and life. Each year, I like to create a dollar value for each hour of my time and then weigh all other things against that particular hourly rate. For instance, if you value your time at $30/hour and you can get someone to mow your lawn for $25/hour, why would you mow your own lawn?

When I started PFSbrands out of my home more than twenty years ago, I was busy running from location to location selling programs, delivering products, buying products, and trying to manage all of the day-to-day duties that every start-up business owner has to deal with. As my business scaled, I consistently had to adjust to the changes and decide where best to focus my time. Today, I'm consumed with speaking, traveling, shows, meetings, emails, business development, overall strategy, and mostly helping to develop ways to make our employee-owners and customers more successful.

As a servant leader and as the CEO of a high-growth company, a large portion of my workload comes from within me. I have a strong desire to create more opportunities for our employee-owners. I've come to realize that to be an effective leader and create a solid work-life balance, I need to consistently work on time management.

Over the last few years I have really focused on taking my time back and not letting workload control me. For you entrepreneurs out there that love what you do, you can relate to the challenges involved with implementing an "ideal" work-life balance. You have to be able to say NO if you want to get control of your time. When you agree to every meeting, take every phone call, get lost in email threads, and respond immediately to every email, before you know it your day is over and you really haven't accomplished anything that moves your business forward. As they say, you're working IN your business, not ON your business and this can become a hard habit to break … but it's doable.

Here is a five-step process for developing the time-management habits that will eventually get you working on your business instead of living in it. These five steps are not just for business leaders; they can help any individual to better manage their time.

1. Decide what's important

First things first, what are two to three processes you can put in place or projects you can finish that will have the greatest impact on your business? Not JUST your business, but also your bottom line. I'm sure there are things you have been putting off because even though you know they will improve your business they just seem like too big of an undertaking. Work with your team to list out all of the things that have the potential to greatly impact your profitability. After listing all of these things, decide on the top two or three and schedule time each day to work on these priorities.

2. Stop doing tasks—delegate or automate

One thing many people who run their own business are proud of is the length of their to-do list. Like it's a badge of honor. It's not. I guarantee almost 75 percent of the tasks on your list can be done by someone else, and in most cases, someone else can do it better than you. In many cases, items on your to-do list can be automated. I'm sure your to-do list is full of remedial tasks that you think YOU have to do. You don't.

For any leader, I believe that a "stop-doing list" is far more important than a to-do list. It's time to stop doing these tasks altogether or delegate these tasks to others. This will free up your time to work on

> For any leader, I believe that a "stop-doing list" is far more important than a to-do list.

what's most important. Don't have any employees? There are many great virtual assistant (VA) services out there to help you out. Just Google "virtual assistants" and you will find numerous options. Posting your content to social media? Delegate it. Sending follow-up emails? Automate it. Editing content? Delegate it. The list goes on and on. There are so many ways to free up your valuable time.

3. Start on the most important thing first (instead of putting it off)

After you've delegated (or automated) many of the tasks on your list, work on what's most important. It can be daunting to start on a big company-altering project.

One strategy to get started is using the methods described in *10 Minute Time Management: The Stress-Free Guide to Getting Stuff Done,* by Ric Thompson. Essentially, if you have a massive project you're putting off, just schedule time on your calendar to work on it ten minutes each day. These small time blocks can add up (and usually last more than ten minutes once you get into them) as you work to complete your project. It's a mind-mastery strategy that could pay off for you.

4. Learn to say NO

As I mentioned earlier, if you work in a company that is growing, at some point you will find yourself spread way too thin. The demands on your time will become endless. It is imperative that you learn to say NO. You can't be everywhere at once nor can you be in every meeting, so learn to delegate and trust your employees. This can be extremely difficult for most business owners, especially founding business owners. It's hard to say no when you want to be a part of everything about your business but it will pay huge dividends in the long run. It will allow you to really focus on what's important for your business—growing it. One great book that really drives this home is *Essentialism: The Disciplined Pursuit of Less,* by Greg McKeown. As the book title implies, it's essentially self-discipline.

5. Block out time for self-improvement and life needs

As you work toward delegating and saying no, another way to manage your time is to block out time on your digital calendar for self-improvement and life needs. Let's face it, when you're pinched for time what goes out the window first? Training, reading, writing, eating, workouts, family time, etc. All of these self-improvement practices and vital life needs usually get pushed to the back burner in exchange for business tasks. I actually went through a period of about three years when I rarely ate anything until dinner, no breakfast or lunch. This wasn't healthy. Take your time back and schedule one to three hours each day for the important things. Always make sure this time is blocked out on your digital calendar so your team realizes it's off limits. Today, I block time for lunch every day. It sounds crazy to some. However, my schedule is so hectic and demanding that if I don't do that, I will simply work through lunch.

In reality, time management is a form of self-discipline. This has been a challenge for me. Like most entrepreneurs, I started my own business because I didn't want the "structure" typically involved with working for others. However, as my companies have scaled, I've found that daily structure and routines have allowed me to be more effective as a leader and that same structure has helped to create a better work-life balance. If you want to grow your business, you must do the following:

- Have the self-discipline to decide what's most important

- Stop doing remedial tasks

- Start doing important tasks

- Say no to unwanted meetings and other requests for your time

Block out manageable chunks of time to accomplish the things that will make you a better person. You can be far more productive if you create a one-hour block of time, versus six ten-minute sections. You built your business and career from the ground up. You did this with persistence, determination, and passion. Where it will go from here is up to your self-discipline, which allows you to take your time back.

THE FUTURE OF PFSBRANDS

Scaling takes vision. At PFSbrands, we have both a ten- and twenty-year vision. Most companies are not thinking that far out, but that can be a fatal flaw.

We feel we can grow at 15 to 25 percent year over year, so if we were going to put a real target out there, a minimum of 15 percent each year for the next twenty years, then we feel very confident in our ability to scale up to 2,000 employees, 20,000 retail customers, and $1 billion in sales.

And this is a conservative estimate based on organic growth. These growth figures don't consider that we may have acquisitions or other business ventures that we may develop. This can be done with our existing business model. We have some great examples of companies that have achieved similar scaling, so we know our projections are realistic. Take a look at Subway, Starbucks, McDonald's, and many other food franchises that have navigated through the growth challenges. In order to scale you have to first BELIEVE, and then you have to EXECUTE.

Starbucks Growth History[27]			PFSbrands Growth Vision		
YEAR	NUMBER OF BRANDED LOCATIONS	GROWTH PERCENTAGE	YEAR	NUMBER OF BRANDED LOCATIONS	GROWTH PERCENTAGE
1991	116		2018	1,349	
1992	165	42.2%	2019	1,548	14.8%
1993	272	64.8%	2020	1,780	15.0%
1994	425	56.3%	2021	2,047	15.0%
1995	677	59.3%	2022	2,354	15.0%
1996	1,015	49.9%	2023	2,708	15.0%
1997	1,412	39.1%	2024	3,114	15.0%
1998	1,886	33.6%	2025	3,581	15.0%
1999	2,498	32.4%	2026	4,118	15.0%
2000	3,501	40.2%	2027	4,736	15.0%
2001	4,709	34.5%	2028	5,446	15.0%
2002	5,886	25.0%	2029	6,263	15.0%
2003	7,225	22.7%	2030	7,202	15.0%
2004	8,569	18.6%	2031	8,283	15.0%
2005	10,241	19.5%	2032	9,525	15.0%
2006	12,440	21.5%	2033	10,954	15.0%
2007	15,011	20.7%	2034	12,597	15.0%
2008	16,680	11.1%	2035	14,486	15.0%
2009	16,635	-0.3%	2036	16,659	15.0%
2010	16,858	1.3%	2037	19,158	15.0%
2011	17,033	1.0%	2038	22,032	15.0%

27   "Starbucks Company Timeline," Starbucks, accessed May 7, 2019, https://www.starbucks.com/assets/ba6185aa2f9440379ce0857d89de8412. pdf; "Number of Starbucks Stores Worldwide from 2003 to 2018," Statistia, November 2018, https://www.statista.com/statistics/266465/ number-of-starbucks-stores-worldwide/.

STEP UP TO THE PLATE
Turning Ideas into Action

As I wrote this book, I did more historical thinking than I've ever done. This project forced me out of my comfort zone and forced me to remember things that I thought I'd forgotten.

At times I wonder where we'd be now if I'd known twenty years ago what I know today. I'm not sure we'd be anywhere close to where we are today if that was the case. On the other hand, we could potentially be miles ahead of where we are today. One thing is for sure: we'll never know because you can't rewrite history.

As I reflect back on my success and as I've studied about others' successes, one thing is certain: there is no such thing as an overnight success.

Scaling is a process, not a destination. If you really want to scale, you need to be constantly moving, constantly evaluating, constantly improving. You need to bring on more talent and better talent. You need the capital required for explosive growth. You need to take back your time.

Items to consider:

1. Is your company scaling upward or coasting downward? Do you have a plan for changing course?

2. What do you need to let go of?

3. What are you doing to continuously improve? At work? At home?

4. Take the five-step process to manage your time better.

5. Who's on your team that needs to go?

6. Are you a leader that needs help scaling your business? See www.grittbusinesscoaching.com.

7. Write a brief biography of your business five years into the future. What are the size, the types of customers it serves, the quality of team members, and your role in the business? Does that picture of the business five years out differ from the one you run or work for today?

Helping Others Become More Successful: Some Closing Words of Wisdom

In the end, what matters most in life are the depth of your relationships with friends and family; and the sheer number of people you've helped along the way. These represent true measures of wealth. Financial wealth, then, is seen as a resource for fostering your relationships.

VERNE HARNISH

Somebody asked me once, "How would you like your epitaph to read?" I'd never thought about that before. However, as I reflected on the question, my answer became clear. I'd want it to read: "Shawn had incredible work ethic and drive. He cared deeply about people and he always expected a lot out of them. He was always encouraging them to be better. Shawn loved his family more than anything and he loved business. He had a lot of fun and

235

throughout his life he worked to help a lot of other people become more successful."

I think that's why I am so passionate about one of my recent business ventures: GRITT Business Coaching (www.grittbusiness-coaching.com). It is designed to help business owners, founders, leaders, and employees become more successful in work and in life by learning how to perfect the process of Keeping Score. GRITT Business Coaching isn't your typical "consulting" company. The company has a solid foundation of talented partners and we're dedicated to changing a lot of lives.

As I reflect back on my high school days, I was fortunate to have some great coaches in basketball and baseball. These coaches had different styles and different approaches, and they made a bigger impact on my life than they did my athletic ability. These coaches saw something in me even at an early age. They saw that I enjoyed being challenged more than most. They always challenged me to work harder than others, even when I was already outworking many. They didn't push me to be better than someone else, they pushed me to always improve over what I did previously.

> When you get serious about becoming more successful, find a coach.

The ability to be coachable is important for anyone that wants to become more successful. Regardless of what you are doing, coaches can help you improve your "game." So many entrepreneurs miss this point. Many people start their own business and develop egos. Their egos get in the way of continuous improvement because they resist advice (coaching) from others.

When you get serious about becoming more successful, find a coach. Conduct an interview process and hire a coach who fits your personality style and who will help you achieve your goals.

I've become really good at what I do. I've become a good leader, I understand business, I understand numbers, I love starting new ventures, I love growing businesses, I've become great at delegating, and I'm a far better listener than I used to be. With all of that being said, I'm constantly seeking advice from others, leaning on my coaches, and pushing myself to improve my "game."

A big part of my continuous learning process is reading. I had a seasoned business developer tell me a couple years ago that he didn't read books because "they all say the same things." That couldn't be further from the truth, and it's simply an excuse used to deflect accountability to improve himself.

My reading primarily revolves around business and personal improvement. Here's my top twenty list:

1. *Start with Why,* by Simon Sinek

2. *Good to Great,* by Jim Collins

3. *Great by Choice,* by Jim Collins

4. *Scaling Up,* by Verne Harnish

5. *Topgrading,* by Bradford D. Smart

6. *The Great Game of Business,* by Jack Stack

7. *Traction,* by Gino Wickman

8. *Rocket Fuel,* by Gino Wickman and Mark Winters

9. *Ownership Thinking,* by Brad Hams

10. *Hyper Sales Growth,* by Jack Daly

11. *The Sales Playbook,* by Jack Daly and Dan Larson

12. *The Sales Acceleration Formula,* by Mark Roberge

13. *The 10X Rule,* by Grant Cardone

14. *Think Big Act Small,* by Jason Jennings

15. *Grit,* by Angela Duckworth

16. *Small Giants,* by Bo Burlingham

17. *Drive,* by Daniel Pink

18. *The E-Myth Revisited,* by Michael Gerber

19. *Extreme Ownership: How U.S. Navy SEALs Lead & Win,* by Jacko Willink and Leif Babin

20. *Switch: How to Change Things When Change Is Hard,* by Chip Heath and Dan Heath

As I look back on nearly fifty years of life, I have a lot to be thankful for. Much of this I attribute to the great teachers, mentors, and coaches I've elected to learn from. This is why I am so passionate about GRITT Business Coaching and helping others become more successful in work and in life.

I've experienced so much in life and in business. I experienced a period where I was so consumed by the day-to-day aspects of business that my entire world was a blur. I was trying to carry the entire weight of the world on my shoulders and wasn't allowing others to step up and excel. I was involved in way too many decisions and wasn't leading in a way that was scalable.

There's nothing more rewarding than coaching others to be better. The financial results are staggering, but the personal results of implementing best practices is even more rewarding. When people thank you for "changing their life," now that's powerful. I know it can happen because I've lived it. I've made the transformation from working IN the business to working ON the business.

When I decided to get my pilot's license, I didn't go out and try to find a nonpilot to teach me. I didn't go out looking for the cheapest route either. Much like everything else I do, I take piloting very seriously. I want to be the best CEO pilot there is so I'm constantly working to get better. I still get instruction and recurrent training because every time I take off in that airplane, I want to ensure I have a successful landing.

Today, any time I'm "stuck" on something, I turn to a book or a coach to help. I know that the right information or the right individual can expedite any opportunity that exists.

STEP UP TO THE PLATE
Turning Ideas into Action

Think about those that have been most influential in your life and take some time to thank them. Take some time to consider how you can impact the lives of others and truly develop those meaningful relationships. Work to learn something new every day and be thankful for the opportunities you have. If you are not exactly where you want to be, stop making excuses and take action to make a better life for yourself. BELIEVE in yourself, think BIG, set GOALS, and COMMIT to becoming more successful in your own life.

Questions to consider:

1. How do you want your epitaph to read?

2. Where are you stuck? Who can help you?

3. Who were your best teachers, mentors, or coaches and why?

4. What books are you going to read in the next six months?

5. What are you doing to improve yourself personally and professionally?

6. Do you know how to land the airplane safely?

7. Are you coachable? Really, are you coachable?

GRITT Business Coaching

If you want to be a better person, you need to surround yourself with better people. If you want to be a better company, you need to surround yourself with better companies.

SHAWN BURCHAM

The coaching concept hit home with me while my team and I were attending several national conferences over the years. In listening to various speakers, meeting different people, hearing some of the questions asked, and engaging in conversations during social hours, we realized we had successfully developed something truly special. Our business model at PFSbrands was undeniably unique compared to many other businesses—a mature and highly functioning culture, an Open-Book Management style, a team of deeply engaged team members (now employee-owners) who care, have fun, and thrive on being accountable to high expectations. We had what every single founder, leader, and C-level executive wanted—a complete and committed team thinking and acting like owners.

From the *Harvard Business Review*:[28]

The Coaching Industry: A Work in Progress, by Ram Charan

> There's no question that future leaders will need constant coaching. As the business environment becomes more complex, they will increasingly turn to coaches for help in understanding how to act. The kind of coaches I am talking about will do more than influence behaviors; they will be an essential part of the leader's learning process, providing knowledge, opinions, and judgment in critical areas. These coaches will be retired CEOs or other experts from universities, think tanks, and government.[29]

Through some of the conferences we were attending, we met many companies that were leaning toward employee-ownership as the solution, believing it would be the magic bullet to creating the perfect culture. Undoubtedly, most of these companies had already implemented an ESOP, yet still hadn't seen a difference in the way their employees acted. To us, it was clear. We knew we couldn't have a successful ESOP unless we increased the level of financial literacy and educate the team on what business is really about. It bears repeating the question—how can we expect our players to win a game when they don't know the rules, and when they know virtually nothing about Keeping Score? As we developed our coaching company, we learned that most companies, ESOP or not, do not share financials outside of a select group of leaders. Many times, this group is only the CFO, CEO, key family members, or company leaders. It seemed obvious to me that you couldn't just "tell" employees the score and expect that they would understand the concept of ownership. It is something that requires a thoughtful approach to education and process. As I

28 Diane Coutu and Carol Kauffman, "What Can Coaches Do for You?" *Harvard Business Review*, January 2009,

29 Ibid.

learned in all my reading, the best business practices rely on patterns and practices to reinforce company and cultural beliefs.

Through these conversations with other company leaders, I realized that what we have achieved at PFSbrands is truly unique. We established this high-engagement culture well before the ESOP. While I'm a big proponent of ESOPs, I also realize they are not the right path for every company. However, establishing a highly involved and active employee base is something every owner or leader should be interested in. At PFSbrands, we have taken the best ideas from leaders across the globe and wrapped them up into a business system that helps leaders to create better alignment and engagement. To accomplish this we created GRITTrac, a cloud technology that allows visibility throughout the entire organization.

For me, PFSbrands is one of those shining examples of a company that proves that high-quality hard work and a caring culture is the best approach in running a business. A responsible and accountable leadership team, along with engaged employees who are financially literate and committed to Keeping Score, produces tremendous results and overwhelming success.

There are all types of challenges in business:

- A disengaged workforce
- Trouble recruiting or retaining employees
- No growth or even declining growth
- Cash flow challenges
- Profitability challenges
- Chaotic growth
- Lack of solid leadership
- Infighting among employees or key leaders
- Lack of systems and processes
- Lack of visibility

- Lack of financial literacy
- No strategic plan
- No goals or no visibility to goals
- Lack of buy-in from the team
- No visibility to key performance indicators (or no key performance indicators at all)
- Siloed or self-interested teams not focused on the good of the company
- And many more

The fact is, there's not a singular answer and there's usually not a quick answer or easy action plan. But there is an *effective* answer. Businesses must become *effective* before they can become *efficient*. And that's exactly why GRITT Business Coaching was formed—to help you find effective answers and successfully scale your business. With services ranging across business strategy, leadership training, employee engagement, KPI development, goal setting, and accounting, GRITT Business Coaching has you covered if you are passionate about creating that high-engagement culture and developing your team into a group of winners that produce consistent results. GRITT Business Coaching was founded by five business partners and 130+ employee-owners who are obsessed with helping others to become more successful in their own lives while helping businesses scale to the next level.

GRITT BUSINESS COACHING NEXT-LEVEL FEATURES

Engage Your Workforce

Ask any president or CEO throughout the nation what their biggest problem is and many will likely answer with: "I don't have enough time to get everything done." What they don't realize is that this statement really means they don't have an engaged workforce. In many cases they don't have a solid leadership team in place or if they do, they likely have a couple key leaders that don't "get it." Consistent Gallup polls and others indicate that 70 percent of the workforce is disengaged.[30] Simply put, these employees just show up. GRITT Business Coaching can show you how to engage your workforce, reduce turnover, and improve loyalty.

When I look for great coaches, I typically want to find someone who has real-world experience. I want someone who has "been there and done it." So many coaches out there today don't truly have the experience, much less a "living lab" like PFSbrands, where you can use our proprietary tools and learn how you can leverage them to improve your business. At PFSbrands, we researched many technology platforms in an effort to align our entire organization with our strategic plan, quarterly objectives, personal goal setting, and many other best practices that I had either developed or learned from my research. As a leader, I wanted something that gave me solid visibility throughout the company, while providing a useful tool for my leaders and all employees. This is not a tool that encourages a leader to be a micromanager, but rather a macromanager. Creating visibility is a tool that helps your employees take accountability and helps your

---

30 Jim Harter, "Dismal Employee Engagement Is a Sign of Global Mismanagement," Gallup, accessed April 9, 2019, https://www.gallup.com/workplace/231668/dismal-employee-engagement-sign-global-mismanagement.aspx.

managers know when to lean in and when to lean out. As we searched for a technology solution, it became apparent that we had developed a business system that was so unique, we were unable to find a technology that worked for PFSbrands. We had such a unique combination of caring, goal setting, and accountability that we decided to develop our own solution.

As the CEO of a highly engaged culture, and thanks to the help of many at PFSbrands, our team has developed a unique program called GRITTrac, a program accessible to everyone in the organization. It houses our entire strategic plan and provides clear line of sight to all company, team, and quarterly goals. It also provides the employees visibility to develop business literacy while enabling the C-team to lead versus micromanage. This complete visibility throughout the entire organization is easily processed by viewing the customized scoreboards.

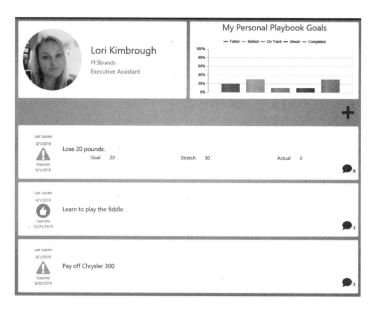

One of the coolest features of GRITTrac is a confidential area that allows individuals to set their own personal goals. In this area, each individual can create goals for their personal life while having a place to constantly track them and keep them visible. This was a good way for me to ensure that the organization was truly focused on our core purpose of helping others in both business and in life. Yes, we're Keeping Score at PFSbrands!

Going to a Level-5 Leader

Going from a level-3 leader up to a level-5 leader could make a huge difference in your career and the lives of those you lead. Learn how to command a room, increase employee loyalty, and improve your overall leadership abilities! When you become a level-5 leader, you have to lead with self-accountability first. This creates an environment that has permission to do the same.

Successful company growth is dependent on the capabilities of its leaders. A company can only grow as far as its top leaders' capabilities. As discussed earlier, it's always great to promote from within when possible. In order to do this, your company MUST provide continuing education and opportunities for your people to learn and grow. With this being said, too many companies spend thousands of dollars to send their employees to trainings. Personal growth starts with training, but in order for people to continuously develop, they have to be encouraged and allowed to "practice." Developing a culture of continuous learning and continuous improvement is critical to retain your staff and provide them with advancement opportunities.

Business and Financial Literacy

From the normal "blocking and tackling" needed in businesses to income statements to cash flow to even setting up an ESOP, we have the experience to improve your business and financial literacy throughout your organization! We even use a business-simulation board game to make it easy and fun to train others on the income statement, balance sheet, and cash flow statement. More than five hundred thousand people have experiential learning as a result of playing this game, implemented through companies like Harley-Davidson, Spirit, and American Electric Power. We have found this board game to be one of the best ways to make business education fun and it is now available to others through GRITT Business Coaching.

Through years of experience we've found it extremely beneficial to use multiple ways to help your team become more business literate. It takes multiple strategies and focus on repetitive instruction to provide your team with the ability to think and act like owners.

The GRITT business simulation board game.

GRITTrac App

Start Keeping Score with an enterprise version of our cloud-based software platform GRITTrac (www.grittrac.com), the only app tailored to your business and team needs. As mentioned earlier, this app has been completely developed internally at PFSbrands and built for commercialization. It's been tried and tested internally and is now available to businesses around the world to help them more effectively communicate company strategy, goals, and overall accountability.

The Dream Team

With 119 collective years of industry experience, $875 million in combined highest-grossing revenue years, and 80 collective years of leadership and coaching experience, meet the ultimate dream team in teaching businesses not only how to start Keeping Score, but how to WIN!

SHAWN BURCHAM, FOUNDER

Shawn Burcham is the founder and CEO of Pro Food Systems, Inc. (PFSbrands), which he and his wife, Julie, started out of their home in 1998. PFSbrands is 100 percent employee-owned, with over 130 employee-owners residing in eighteen different states. The company has more than 1,400 branded food-service locations across forty states and they are best known for their Champs Chicken franchise brand, which was started in 1999. The company now offers BluTaco as a franchise brand and Cooper's Express as a license program. They also create private-label programs for many of their customers. PFSbrands works predominately with supermarkets and convenience stores across the country.

Prior to starting PFSbrands, Shawn spent five years with a Fortune 100 company, Mid-America Dairyman, pioneering an intern program and sales training program. At a young age just after graduating college he assumed a fourteen-state regional sales manager position for the Packaged and Processed Cheese Division. He went on to spend three years as a regional sales manager for a Midwest Chester Fried distributor.

Shawn made a decision in 1998 to take a major risk in quitting his job and starting a business from the ground floor. Since starting PFSbrands, Shawn has started and grown more than ten businesses, while also investing in other businesses where he feels he can help owners become more successful.

It's because of these varied experiences that Shawn truly believes empowering employees to think and act like owners is the recipe for success.

Shawn is passionate about helping others become more successful in work and in life. He believes in taking care of employees and providing them with opportunities where they can excel. He has a nonentitlement mentality and a straight talk approach. He believes that all leaders need to CARE, HAVE FUN, and HOLD PEOPLE ACCOUNTABLE TO HIGH EXPECTATIONS. Shawn is a true entrepreneur that has taken the risks necessary to lead a company to double-digit growth for twenty-plus years.

PATRICK CARPENTER, PRESIDENT

Patrick's thirty-year career includes senior management positions with two global Fortune 100 companies and international business assign-

ments in Canada, Brazil, and Mexico. Patrick also co-owned his own medical business, which he grew from $1 million in revenue to over $12 million in revenue in four years.

During his career, he developed more than $300 million in new business. He has worked with companies such as McKesson, Johnson & Johnson, TYCO, 3M, Novartis, and New Belgium, as well as public institutions such as Johns Hopkins University and the Mayo Clinic. During one three-year assignment with Omron Healthcare, Patrick helped lead the professional medical group to acquire the American Heart Association endorsement for a new blood pressure monitor, commercializing the endorsement with physicians nationwide. Patrick also spent personal time to advance awareness in hypertension working with leaders from the American Heart Association.

Patrick is the son of the late Jill Carpenter, who helped to pioneer the concept of Open-Book Management, coauthoring two books, *The Power of Open-Book Management* and *The Field Book of Open-Book Management,* and is currently working on two books that are certain to bring honor to his late, great mother as well as GBC. Patrick's life work is now dedicated to honoring the legacy of Jill and the thousands of employees who are just crazy enough to believe that all employees should be treated with unconditional positive regard and taught to understand the financial rules of business and to use what they learn to benefit them at home.

JENNIFER BRIGGS, PARTNER

Jennifer Briggs brings more than two decades of practice in human resources, organizational development, and executive leadership from a variety of industries. She served as VP of Human Resources with

New Belgium Brewing for twelve years, which due to her direct efforts has been named a Worldblu company since 2005, received the honor nine times by *Outside* magazine as one of the best places to work (even beating Google in 2008), and was ranked in 2008 by the *Wall Street Journal* as being among the top small workplaces in the US. Currently, Jennifer serves as an educator and advisor to companies who want to redefine value in a more holistic manner. Building healthy, profitable, democratically managed companies with shared capital ownership is her passion. A mentor once taught her to never let a rule get in the way of making a good decision and she strives to make critical thinking, intention, and agile action guiding principles. She brings a nontraditional HR viewpoint of relying primarily on values, communication, and community.

She is an advisor with the Beyster Institute with the University of California San Diego and serves on corporate boards for PFSbrands, GISinc., and Engineering Economics, Inc. She is on the advisory boards for the Moxie Exchange and the Colorado State University Business School, and participates with the Democracy at Work Institute. She holds a master of science in organizational leadership, graduate studies in enterprise project management, and a bachelor of science in community health education. She is currently a fellow with the Institute for the Study of Employee-Ownership and Profit Sharing at Rutgers University, a distinction as one of only twenty-two research fellows enlisted to advance the study of broad-based employee stock ownership, equity compensation, gain sharing, profit sharing, and worker cooperatives.

MARK GANDY, PARTNER

Mark Gandy founded G3CFO and Free Agent CFO and he is obsessed with helping businesses grow their three bottom lines—top-line unit sales, profitable cash flow, and the street value of the organizations they are trying to grow. As a nontraditional CFO, Mark

uses his acumen of marketing, sales management, streamlined operating workflows, data analytics, and agile-based business modeling to support these objectives.

While Mark doesn't necessarily "advertise" CEO coaching, he has a unique gift of helping CEOs better lead their company forward. He can work alongside an existing CFO or serve a much-needed CFO role in organizations that have a vacancy or have not quite become large enough to warrant a full-time CFO.

Mark is honored, humbled, and thrilled to be a part of the GBC ownership group, whose primary aim is to move the companies they serve closer to their true calling—great results for their customers, their internal teams, and the communities they live in.

TREVOR MONNIG, PARTNER

Trevor Monnig has spent more than fifteen years in the role of CFO for two high-growth companies in the manufacturing and distribution industry. He currently serves as the CFO for PFSbrands, where he has been instrumental in elevating financial awareness and overall employee engagement. He prides himself on being a progressive CFO that goes above and beyond the traditional finance roles. Trevor is passionate about integrating the entire organization to align all business units to company goals. He recognizes people as the company's biggest asset and leverages this by hiring for culture and nurturing healthy working relationships. He is experienced in deploying Open-Book Management and firmly believes this transparent platform is the future of organizational management.

As CFO of PFSbrands, a 100 percent ESOP company, Trevor educates all teams on financial performance, financial literacy, factors impacting the business, and connecting each employee-owner to the profitability of the company. He promotes data in all decision-making, encourages exploration, and has a tolerance for failure. He serves on the corporate board of PFSbrands and other companies while also being highly active in the ESOP and Open-Book Management communities.

The Art of Coaching

There are numerous consultants and coaches in the world. However, very few of them are focused on engaging the heads, hands, and hearts of all employees. Further, few come with this type of experience and leading-edge technology to simplify implementation and maintain visibility, along with a "living lab" that continues to innovate and improve on a consistent basis.

Too many consultants and coaches want to put you in a "box," and they want to teach you to do things exactly the same way. Our approach and belief at GRITT Business Coaching is much different. In fact, it's why PFSbrands is where we are today. I was not a proponent of ONE system. I know I've mentioned this several times, but it can't be overstated: we've taken the *best* systems and processes from the *best* thought leaders in the world and combined them to create a high-level "systems approach" to running businesses. We customize our approach for each company based upon their needs and desires. No two companies are alike, and we feel it is important to remain somewhat flexible as we coach to implement change in each organization we work with.

> We've taken the *best* systems and processes from the *best* thought leaders in the world and combined them to create a high-level "systems approach" to running businesses.

If you're ready to take your business into the future and harness our decades of experience, contact us today. From ESOPs to engaging your workforce to Open-Book Management to accounting to everything in between, GRITT Business Coaching can help hone your leadership skills. Our five-step system will provide you with the tools needed to start Keeping Score so that you can WIN!

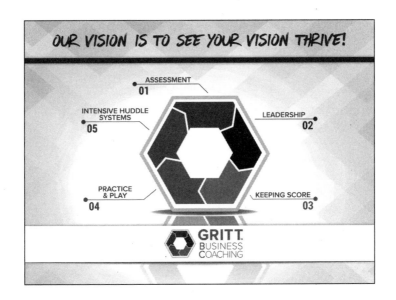

VISIT www.grittbusinesscoaching.com

PHONE 1 (833) GO GRITT (464-7488)

EMAIL info@GRITTbusinesscoaching.com

ADDRESS PO Box 580, Holts Summit, MO 65043

ACKNOWLEDGMENTS

There's a huge irony with the existence of this book. As a child, and even through my educational years, I despised reading and writing. I have to thank my wife, Julie, for helping me to become a better writer over the years. She taught high school business, but unlike me, she enjoyed reading and writing.

I met Mark Gandy when I was forty years old. Thanks to Mark, I have become an avid reader and I now enjoy writing as well. Mark consistently asked me to consider writing a book as he learned more about my journey.

As you have learned throughout this book, there are a lot more people that played important roles in conceiving this book. As an avid reader now, I have mentors that don't even know me. All of the teachers, coaches, mentors, bosses, and coworkers I've had over the years have been instrumental in making this happen.

Finally, after I met Jack Daly in February of 2018, I was determined to finish this book. When Jack and I met, he had just recently lost his longtime friend and spouse to cancer. I was fortunate enough to sit through his sessions and have lunch with him on two occasions. While I was trying to learn from Jack, he was doing the same with me. I was amazed that he thought my story was interesting enough for him to encourage me to write a book. His "get it done" attitude and "no excuses" approach were inspiring and relatable to me. I reached out to him a few weeks later to learn more about how he published his books. Thanks for the advice and the nudge, Jack.

ABOUT THE AUTHOR

Shawn Burcham is the founder and CEO of Pro Food Systems, now commonly referred to as PFSbrands. After working two prior jobs in the food service industry, Shawn decided to take a big risk and start a business of his own. Shawn and his wife, Julie, started PFSbrands shortly after having their first child. Taking a major risk and going "all in," they went from a double-income, no-kid family to a no-income, one-kid family in order to start their American dream.

Starting with nothing from his garage in Willard, Missouri, Shawn developed Champs Chicken and started selling fryers, hot cases, chicken breading, batter dip, shortening, and packaging. Since that time, many more products have been developed and PFSbrands has been able to maintain double-digit growth over the last twenty years, while building a business that has a national footprint. While doing all of this, Shawn has created a company culture that has been recognized consistently on a national level as a Great Place to Work, and the company's growth has been recognized by *Inc.* for nine years straight as one of the fastest growing privately held companies in America. PFSbrands was recognized by Forbes Small Giants as one of the Best Small Companies of 2019.

While Shawn still serves as CEO of PFSbrands, over the last

twenty years he has started or invested in over ten companies while migrating through several acquisitions. In January of 2017, he created an employee stock ownership plan (ESOP) in order to transfer 100 percent ownership of PFSbrands to his current and future employees. PFSbrands is now an employee-owned company. Shawn is proud to offer this unique ESOP opportunity for his employees to earn shares of ownership without paying for them, and without assuming the many risks that most business owners are typically required to take.

Shawn has been able to migrate through the challenges of growth over the years because of his drive, determination, and GRITT, along with a unique set of core values he lives by, as defined by his HAPPINESS RULE. He exudes a positive attitude at all times, he believes in straight talk communication, he expects a lot out of people, and he is adamantly opposed to entitlements. If you have the opportunity to meet Shawn or hear him speak, you'd never guess him to be introverted. However, he considers himself an introverted blue-collar individual that has the ability and business acumen to relate to top-level executives and employees at all levels within organizations. He believes everyone should work hard and play hard. In every interview he conducts, he consistently lets people know that he cares, he has fun, and he has high expectations while holding people accountable to those expectations. Shawn is an avid goal setter. He thinks big and he has an uncanny ability to commit to reaching these goals, while inspiring others to do the same. He believes in creating visibility and Keeping Score in life and in business.

OUR SERVICES

For additional GRITT resources and to learn more about Shawn Burcham, go to www.shawnburcham.com. Subscribe to Shawn's blog and follow him on social media to stay current on the latest tips, concrete tools, and best practices to improve your business performance. To learn more about speaking engagements, email him directly at info@shawnburcham.com.

If you're ready to start Keeping Score and implementing these strategies with GRITT, consult GRITT Business Coaching (GBC) at www.grittbusinesscoaching.com. Offering six key services to help move your business strategy forward—including our proprietary GRITTrac goal -tracking software (www.grittrac.com)—GBC will tailor a custom plan that is right for your organization.

To see how these strategies can be put into action and learn more about the "living lab," visit www.pfsbrands.com. With a core purpose of helping others become more successful in work and in life, PFSbrands provides not only high-quality food service programs and support to retailers, but a variety of marketing tools (blog, QSR Nation podcast, social media) for any retailer in the QSR space. More information on its franchise brands can be found at www.champschicken.com and www.theblutaco.com.